"Stamped with the Image of God"

American Catholic Identities
A Documentary History
Christopher J. Kauffman, General Editor

American Catholic Identities is a nine-volume series that makes available to the general reader, the student, and the scholar seminal documents in the history of American Catholicism. Subjects are wide-ranging and topically ordered within periods to encounter the richly textured experiences of American Catholics from the earliest years to the present day. The twenty-six editors of these volumes reveal a command of trends in historiography since the publication of John Tracy Ellis's three-volume work, *Documents of American Catholic History*. Hence the American Catholic Identities series shows developments in our understanding of social history — the significance of gender, race, regionalism, ethnicity, and spirituality, as well as Catholic thought and practice before and since the Second Vatican Council.

The series elucidates myriad meanings of the American Catholic experience by working with the marker of religious identity. It brings into relief the historical formations of religious self-understandings of a wide variety of Catholics in a society characterized by the principles of religious liberty, separation of church and state, religious pluralism, and voluntarism.

American Catholic Identities is united by such dominant factors in American history as waves of immigration, nativism, anti-Catholicism, racism, sexism, and several other social and ideological trends. Other aspects of unity are derived from American Catholic history: styles of episcopal leadership, multiple and various types of Catholic institutions, and the dynamic intellectual interaction between the United States and various national centers of Catholic thought. Woven into the themes of this documentary history are the protean meanings of what constitutes being American and Catholic in relation to the formations of religious identities.

Titles of books in the series are:

Public Voices: Catholics in the American Context, Steven M. Avella and Elizabeth McKeown

The Frontiers and Catholic Identities, Anne M. Butler, Michael E. Engh, S.J., and Thomas W. Spalding, C.F.X.

Creative Fidelity: U.S. Catholic Intellectual Identities, Scott Appleby, Patricia Byrne, C.S.J., and William Portier

Keeping Faith: European and Asian Catholic Immigrants, Jeffrey M. Burns, Ellen Skerrett, and Joseph M. White

Prayer and Practice in the American Catholic Community, Joseph P. Chinnici, O.F.M., and Angelyn Dries, O.S.F.

Gender Identities in American Catholicism, Paula Kane, James Kenneally, and Karen Kennelly, C.S.J.

"Stamped with the Image of God": African Americans as God's Image in Black, Cyprian Davis, O.S.B., and Jamie Phelps, O.P.

¡Presente! U.S. Latino Catholics from Colonial Origins to the Present, Timothy Matovina and Gerald E. Poyo, in collaboration with Cecilia González-Andrieu, Steven P. Rodríguez, and Jaime R. Vidal

The Crossing of Two Roads: Being Catholic and Native in the United States, Marie Therese Archambault, O.S.F., Mark G. Thiel, and Christopher Vecsey

A workshop for the editors of these books was entirely funded by a generous grant from the Louisville Institute.

American Catholic Identities
A Documentary History
Christopher J. Kauffman, General Editor

"Stamped with the Image of God"

African Americans
as God's Image in Black

Cyprian Davis, O.S.B.
Jamie Phelps, O.P.
Editors

ORBIS BOOKS
Maryknoll, New York 10545

Founded in 1970, Orbis Books endeavors to publish works that enlighten the mind, nourish the spirit, and challenge the conscience. The publishing arm of the Maryknoll Fathers and Brothers, Orbis seeks to explore the global dimensions of the Christian faith and mission, to invite dialogue with diverse cultures and religious traditions, and to serve the cause of reconciliation and peace. The books published reflect the opinions of their authors and are not meant to represent the official position of the Maryknoll Society. To obtain more information about Maryknoll and Orbis Books, please visit our website at www.maryknoll.org.

Copyright © 2003 by Cyprian Davis, O.S.B., and Jamie Phelps, O.P.

Published by Orbis Books, Maryknoll, New York, U.S.A.

Manufactured in the United States of America

Library of Congress Cataloging-in-Publication Data

Stamped with the image of God : African Americans as God's image in Black / Cyprian Davis, Jamie Phelps, editors.
    p. cm. – (American Catholic identities)
    Includes bibliographical references and index.
    ISBN 1-57075-522-1 (cloth) – ISBN 1-57075-351-2 (pbk.)
    1. African American Catholics–History. I. Davis, Cyprian. II. Phelps, Jamie T. (Jamie Therese), 1941-   III. Series.
    BX1407.N4 S73 2004
    282′.73′08996073 – dc22

                                                                        2003018595

To the memory of
Africa's children in the Americas
who passed on the faith,
walked in hope,
and served with love,
stamped with the image of God

CONTENTS

Part 3
CONGREGATIONS OF BLACK SISTERS

Part 4
THE POST–CIVIL WAR PERIOD

Part 7
MID-CENTURY: WINDS OF CHANGE

Part 8
CIVIL RIGHTS AND
AFRICAN AMERICAN CATHOLICS

Part 9
THE CHURCH ADDRESSES RACISM

Part 10
THE WITNESS OF AFRICAN AMERICAN CATHOLICS: CHALLENGE AND HOPE

FOREWORD

Christopher J. Kauffman

The historical consciousness of the African American Catholic community has expanded considerably over the past forty years. As many historians and theologians have pointed out, the civil rights movement, the Second Vatican Council, and the culture of the 1960s converged to form a new phase in the development of modern consciousness, symbolized by the growth of national organizations and new forms of liturgical music. The Black Catholic Congress of 1987 is emblematic of this growth in historical self-understanding as members of national, diocesan, and parish organizations joined the black Catholic bishops and many religious and diocesan priests to form three days of a community of worship, song, and dialogue. Energized by this experience, representatives met to plan further meetings of the congress. This national meeting has become a permanent feature in the life of the community with a national office to organize and promote the congress movement. During the time of the 1987 congress, Cyprian Davis, O.S.B., a founding member of the Black Catholic Caucus in 1968 (see document 50) and a speaker in the congress twenty years later, was then completing his manuscript of the 1990 book *The History of the Black Catholics in the United States*. Sister Jamie Phelps, O.P., also made a presentation at the congress and had recently embarked on a career in theology. Her specialty is missiology, with particular interest in John R. Slattery, the first superior general of the St. Joseph's Society of the Sacred Heart (Josephites). Because of his role in the ordination of three black Josephite priests and his promotion of the community's charism to minister to African Catholics, Slattery is a significant historical figure.

Many documents in this volume formed the basis for Davis's book. The book was preceded by the publication of articles by him and other scholars. For example, the *U.S. Catholic Historian* published an article by Davis on the black Catholic experience in the nineteenth century that included the account of the five Black Catholic Congresses between 1889 and 1895, the historical precedent of the contemporary congress movement. As editor of this journal, I am pleased to have been associated with this 1986 issue and the one we published on the 1982 congress, as well as other issues on the topic. The 1986 issue was purchased by many directors of the diocesan offices of black Catholic ministry, a sign of both the high demand for historical works and the growth of the national movement of this specialized ministry. These articles were very popular among many people in the pews, which whetted the appetite for more — a hunger that was satisfied by Davis's book, many articles by Jamie Phelps, and others. In a very real sense, the enthusiastic response to this history of the black Catholic people illustrates its role in the dynamic of contemporary identity formation in the African American Catholic community. Central to the development of the black Catholic self-understanding is both its historical and contemporary experiences with racism within the Church, the academy, and society.

The reader will note that many documents gathered by Davis and Phelps clearly evince the salient role of the laity in the history of African American life and thought. Documents of the two principal communities of black women religious, the Oblate Sisters of Providence and the Congregation of the Sisters of the Holy Family (New Orleans), reveal their commitment to various forms of ministry. With only a few black priests to serve this community, these black sisters were vital witnesses and ministers to their own people. There were the three Healy brothers who "passed" for whites and three black Josephite priests, but it was not until after the foundation of St. Augustine's Seminary in Bay St. Louis, Mississippi (1930), by the Society of the Divine Word for black aspirants to the priesthood, that there was a steady flow of diocesan priests into the black parishes (see documents 46 and 47). Augustus Tolton, who was born a slave and ordained a priest in 1886, was the first African American Catholic priest who easily identified with the people (see documents 27, 28, and 29). Hundreds of people displayed their faith-filled appreciation for a priest who knew what it meant to be on the margins of the Church and society.

A distinctive dialectical pattern emerges in these documents charting the development of the black Catholic community of faith. Many documents demonstrate the faith commitment of the people: letters, baptismal records, and speeches of various individuals and communities that reveal an identification as a people "Stamped in the Image of God," in juxtaposition to documents penned by Catholics in leadership positions who tacitly, if not explicitly, deny the social, existential, and religious reality of that image. (There were putatively enlightened white Catholics who referred to the inherent inequality of people of color.)

For example, part 1 features this juxtaposition: placement of a sequence of a devotional society in Spain, baptismal records in Spanish Florida, escaped slaves from the South to join the Spanish black "parish" colony in

Florida, and then the Code Noir that forges the juridical links in the chains of slavery with the alloy of religion.

Part 2 opens with a remarkably proactive 1817 document that was composed by a remarkably proactive group of Catholic "people of color" who requested that the trustees of St. Mary's provide religious education for their children. They were particularly concerned to protect them from those people of "the sects" who were eager to convert them; the proselytizers were most likely representative of the newly formed African Methodist Episcopal Church, founded in Baltimore in 1816, the year before the composition of this letter (see document 7). This is followed by several pieces of correspondence illustrating faith and social commitment, and a letter from a woman to Pope Pius IX complaining about the educational policy of New York's Archbishop John Hughes that neglects provision for her people. The second section of this part juxtaposes two bishops defending slavery with four documents by prominent European laypeople and bishops opposing American slavery as if they were responding to previous statements defending the so-called peculiar institution.

Following in the rich vein of proactive laity are documents on the five Black Catholic Congresses and the remarkable leadership of Daniel Rudd, the founder of the *American Catholic Tribune*, a national black Catholic weekly. These meetings became progressively more critical of the Church's slow pace of social provision and disillusioned with Church leadership on discrimination, but their commentaries were always prefaced by candid expressions of loyalty to the Church (see documents 33–37). The reader will note that Thomas Wyatt Turner is the successor of Rudd in the Society for the Advancement of Colored Catholics and its subsequent Society of Federated Catholics (see document 41).

These societies presage the era of civil rights featured in Part 8. During this time several organizations such as the Clergy Caucus, the Black Sisters Conference, the National Black Catholic Conference, and various other groups representative of black public Catholicism were committed to redressing the historic injustices of racism. Throughout the civil rights era African American voices were in harmony with the general trend of expressing an emphasis on the African dimension of their identity. The period also witnessed the appearance of black Catholic theological reflection and analysis. Part 9, "The Church Addresses Racism," underscores the leadership roles of the black bishops so clearly demonstrated in their pastoral letters and so dramatically manifested in the various African American congresses. Part 10, which reveals the imprint of Sister Jamie Phelps, features reflections by notable activists, such as Father Clarence R. Rivers, the composer, performer, and director of African American music and its integration into the liturgy.

As noted scholars who complement their research and writing with a commitment to practical forms of ministry, Cyprian Davis and Jamie Phelps have assembled documents that reveal the many strands of African Americans' life and thought. They neatly weave these threads into patterns of meaning in their introductions and by assembling them into ten coherent parts. This book has wide appeal for the African American people in the pews; and many hundreds of activists in national, diocesan, and parish spheres; and professors and students throughout academia. Each group will be grateful for this book's contribution to their understanding of the salient themes of African American Catholic historical identities.

ACKNOWLEDGMENTS

The compilation of these documents has been a long and difficult task. We owe a debt of gratitude to very many people in many different places. Yet it is a pleasant task to recall the many persons who have aided us, and we regret that neither time nor space permits us to name them all.

We owe a special debt of gratitude to Christopher Kauffman, our general editor, who had the vision to create this series of historical sources. His encouragement and support were never lacking. Future historians and scholars will be in his debt. We wish to thank also the unceasing efforts of William Burrows at Orbis, whose suggestions and critique were of invaluable aid. We extend our thanks as well to Catherine Costello and all the others at Orbis who made this publication possible. Our sincere thanks in a special way to Father Aelred Cody, O.S.B., of St. Meinrad Archabbey for his work of translation.

To the many who granted permissions and suggestions in libraries and archives both in the United States and abroad, we say sincere thanks. Among them are Monsignor Dewane of the Pontifical Council for Justice and Peace; Father Peter Hogan, S.S.J., of the Josephite Archives; Virginia Meacham Gould of Our Lady of Holy Cross College in New Orleans; Charles Nolan, archivist of the Archdiocesan Archives of New Orleans; Sister Jean Marie Aycock, O.S.U., of the Ursuline Convent Archives of New Orleans; Sister Carolyn Leslie, S.S.F., of the Archives of the Sisters of the Holy Family in New Orleans; Wayne Furman of the New York Public Library Special Collections; William Kevin Cawley of the University of Notre Dame Archives; Abbé G. Leguay of the Archives of the Diocese of Orléans in France; Sister Reginald Gerdes, O.S.P., of the Archives of the Oblate Sisters of Providence; Sister Maria E. McCall, S.B.S., of the Sisters of the Blessed Sacrament Archives; Joseph J. Casino of the Philadelphia Archdiocesan Historical Research Center; Don H. Bushe of the Cincinnati Archdiocesan Archives; Father Paul Thomas of the Archives of the Archdiocese of Baltimore; Father Keith R. Brennan of the St. Augustine Diocesan Archives; Father John W. Bowen, S.S., of the Sulpician Archives in Baltimore; Father Lawrence Lucas of New York City; Father Russell Elmayer, chancellor of the Diocese of Raleigh, North Carolina; Sister Marguerita Smith, O.P., of the Archdiocesan Archives of

New York; Mary Elizabeth Sperry of the U.S. Conference of Catholic Bishops; Father Chester Smith, S.V.D., of the National Black Catholic Clergy Caucus; Walter Hubbard of the National Office for Black Catholics; Sister Patricia Chappell, S.N.D., of the National Black Sisters' Conference; and to all those who gave permission to reprint documents from their publications and periodicals. Finally, these who granted us the use of photographs for this book merit special mention.

INTRODUCTION

The history of black Catholics in the United States extends back to the beginning of Catholicism in what is now the United States. On the other hand, scholarly interest in the history of black Catholics in the United States has a very recent past. It was assumed that the sources of black Catholic history were either nonexistent or of little importance. Today we know that the sources have always been there; it was only a question of uncovering them. As a result, searchers have found that a new and richer treasure of American Church history is gradually being revealed and that much misinformation and misinterpretation is being corrected. The documents, moreover, reveal the many facets of the black Catholic community, and they identify the manifold presence of black Catholics within the American Church.

The collection published here is by no means exhaustive. The choice of documents has been guided by a desire to document the evolution of the African American Catholic community from the Spanish period until the last decade of the twentieth century. Our intention has been to allow each document to speak for itself. An attempt has been made to relate each document to the history of the time.

Part 1

THE SPANISH AND FRENCH PERIOD

Among the Spanish who arrived in this country in 1565, there were black-skinned Spaniards who came as settlers into what some called the New World. Some were slaves; others were free; all were Catholic. At the beginning of the eighteenth century, French settlers arrived at the mouth of the Mississippi River. Others settled along the Gulf. These French settlers began importing African slaves as early as the first quarter of the eighteenth century.

It is not surprising that many of the blacks who came to the Spanish settlement would be Spaniards from the Spanish mainland. By the fourteenth century the kingdoms of Aragon, Leon, and Castile had begun importing black slave labor into Spain. By the end of the century, many were Catholics who played a large part in the daily life of the period. A charter issued by the king of Aragon, John II, legally recognized a brotherhood (*cofradía*) of freed blacks in Barcelona in 1455.[1] The brotherhoods were an important factor in medieval Spanish life, and they would have an extensive role in the evangelization of free blacks and slaves in all Latin America.

1. The Brotherhood of Blessed Mary of the Blacks, Valencia, 1472

The following excerpt translated from Catalan is from a second charter granted to the free blacks of Valencia to form a brotherhood of "Blessed Mary of the Blacks" in 1472. The constitution of the brotherhood is contained within the charter issued by the prince, Ferdinand II, king of Sicily and prince of Castile, the future king of Aragon and spouse of Isabella the Catholic of Castile, who supported Columbus twenty years later.

---

1. "Ordenanzas de la cofradía de los cristianos negros de Barcelona," *Colección de documentos ineditos del Archivo General de la Corona de Aragón*, 109, ed. D. Próspero de Bofarull y Mascaró, 7:465–71.

3

1472, November 13. The Royal Palace of Valencia.
To the brotherhood of Blessed Mary of the Blacks.
We, Ferdinand, etc.

Because it is fitting for the royal majesty that it show favor to its subjects and lead them to observe the bond of charity which is known as the foundation of all good. Therefore, inasmuch as you are black men freed from slavery who desire to have a brotherhood or union in charity, according to the word of Holy Scripture which teaches us to have a union of love and charity among us and to exercise the works of charity, you have respectfully presented to our majesty this new ordinance for the preservation of your brotherhood and union of alms, drawn up as a petition with its articles as follows:

Most Excellent Lord:

The free blacks of the present city of Valencia by the licence and the authority of the deputy of the governor, have been accustomed to gather every year, for the service, honor, and glory of our Lord God and the most holy Virgin Mary, their mother. They have ordained that each year that a waxen candle be made and all together they carry it with much devotion to the chapel of the Virgin Mary of Grace of the monastery of the blessed St. Augustine. And as the aforesaid blacks wish to increase in merits and enthusiasm [*ab sumo studi*] in the service of our Lord God and his aforesaid mother which they cannot conveniently do so unless your royal majesty, given the form and manner, either award the graces and privileges; or we supplicate that the aforesaid free blacks, which are between thirty seven and forty in number might by your worship, Lord, be awarded these following graces and privileges.

First, my Lord, may your worship award to the aforesaid blacks the privilege and the grace to become a *cofradía* [brotherhood] and a society, granting and awarding the licence whereby they might be able to come together and to regulate [their affairs] as many times as this will be good as well as necessary, without the permissions and authority of any judge or official of your majesty, for the utility and the profit of the aforesaid brotherhood and the business thereof.

Secondly, the aforesaid blacks who live in this city who wish to enter into the aforesaid *cofradía* and to be part of it might have the power to elect each year four stewards [*maiorals*], those whom they elect are those who are *cofradía* members, or the major part are such. [The election is to take place] each year at the end of Eastertide.

Again, that the aforesaid stewards [*maiorals*] and *cofradía* members can constitute a syndic [council] which can intervene in all the cases and legal acts of the aforesaid confraternity.

Again, that the same *cofradía* members and stewards might have the authority to buy and to possess a house in the present city of Valencia in which they can assemble and discuss in order to carry out the business and affairs of the aforementioned confraternity and which can be dedicated to the honor and service of the most holy Virgin Mary of Grace.

Again, that the same *cofradía* members and stewards may pass regulations at any time and whenever necessary and useful for the aforementioned confraternity; and if some necessity occurs they can levy a tax and taxes as it seems good to them with the qualification that whatever is ordained by them or the majority of the members should be observed by all.

Again, if by necessity of infirmity, poverty, or misery, some members of the *cofradía* who ... will be placed in circumstances who otherwise will not be able to survive or support their life, these members will be aided by the other ... aforesaid *cofradía* members. ...

Given in the royal palace of Valencia, 13th day of the month of November, 1472. ...

I, Prince and King ...

Miguel Gual Camarena, "Una cofradía de negros libertos en el siglo XV. Documento. 1472 noviembre, 13. Palacio Real de Valencia," *Estudios de Edad Media de la Corona de Aragón*. vol. 5 (Zaragoza, 1952), 457–66, with permission.

2. Ecclesiastical Records of St. Augustine Parish in Florida, 1796, 1812

Among the oldest ecclesiastical records in the United States are the sacramental registers of the church of St. Augustine in Florida. The earliest records begin with the baptisms of the year 1565. Until 1763, the baptisms of all persons regardless of race were kept in the same book. From 1763 to 1784, the Spanish were forced to vacate the colony and move to Cuba following the Seven Years' War. Beginning with 1784, when the Spanish returned to Florida, the sacramental registers for blacks were kept in books now separate from the register of the whites. From the beginning of the eighteenth century, the Spanish governors granted freedom to slaves in the British colonies who ran away and came to Florida and converted to the Catholic faith. Many African slaves born in the colonies reached St. Augustine. The following is a translation from the Spanish of an entry in the book of baptisms for people of color. In this instance it would seem that the baby's parents were already free before they left Georgia.

Sunday, the eighteenth day of December seventeen hundred ninety-six, I, Dr. Miguel Reilly, beneficed curate and vicar, [and] ecclesiastical judge, of this parish church in the Place and Province of Saint Augustine of Florida, baptized and placed the holy oils on a baby of color [*de color moreno*] who was born free on the nineteenth day of November of the current year, the natural son of Abraham MacSuit, a free black man, native of Savannah, and of Isabel Holms, a free black woman, native of the City of Savannah in Georgia, and [I] administered to him the sacred ceremonies and prayers of our holy mother the Church and imposed the name José. His Godparents were: Sisto Lopez, second sergeant of the first company of the third battalion of the Regiment of Cuba, and Teresa Hambly, resident of this city, and I advised them on the spiritual parentage and other obligations. And I sign it on the aforesaid day, month, and year.

Miguel O'Reilly

"The Spanish Colonial Parochial Registers of St. Augustine, Baptisms Colored, 1793–1807, book 2, number 155, Archives of the Diocese of St. Augustine, Jacksonville, Florida, with permission.

The death registers for blacks indicate that many of the soldiers garrisoned in St. Augustine were black, many of them mulattoes, and some, as in the following instance, were African born.

Sunday, the eleventh day of December, eighteen hundred twelve, Francisco de Castro, soldier of the first Company of Black men of the Havana Auxiliaries in this Plaza, a native of Africa son of fathers whose identity is unknown, about forty-four years in age [who] died in communion with our holy mother the Church, having received the Holy Sacraments of Penance, Communion, and Extreme Unction, whose body I, Don Miguel Crosby, holding the office of beneficed assistant and Vicar and Ecclesiastical Judge and this parochial Church, and the province of St. Augustine of Florida, buried in the cemetery of the parish church on the day following his death and I place this name as signature.

Miguel Crosby

"The Spanish Colonial Parochial Registers of St. Augustine, Deaths Colored, 1785–1821," no. 182, with permission.

3. Civil and Ecclesiastical Records of Louisiana: The Code Noir, 1724

The French began to settle the Gulf Coast on what is now Mississippi and Alabama with the establishment of Biloxi in 1699 and Mobile in 1711. New

Orleans was founded in 1718 by Jean-Baptiste Le Moyne de Bienville, who with his brother, Pierre Le Moyne d'Iberville, had opened up Louisiana as a French colony. By the first quarter of the eighteenth century African slaves were imported into Louisiana through New Orleans.

By 1685, Louis XIV, king of France, had promulgated a series of ordinances or rules governing the life and conduct of the African slaves in the French colonies in the Americas. Drawn up under the authority of Jean-Baptiste Colbert, the all-powerful minister of King Louis XIV, these laws, known as the Code Noir, became the slave laws for the French territory in Louisiana and the Gulf Coast. The Code Noir, like the Spanish Slave Code, known as the Siete Partidas of Alfonso X the Wise (1252–84), was based upon the Roman law. These slave codes, unlike the American laws, were based upon the premise that even slaves had certain rights. Nevertheless, although the code assured certain rights, it also contained measures that were very harsh and demeaning. The following excerpt of the Code Noir is based upon the formulation made by Louis XV in 1724.

THE CODE NOIR OR EDICT OF THE KING, SERVING AS REGULATIONS FOR THE GOVERNMENT AND ADMINISTRATION OF JUSTICE, POLICE, DISCIPLINE AND COMMERCE OF NEGRO SLAVES, IN THE PROVINCE AND COLONY OF LOUISIANA

Given at Versailles in the month of March 1724

Louis by the grace of God, king of France and Navarre: to all present and to come. Greetings! The Directors of the Company of the Indies have made known to me that the province and colony of Louisiana is well established by a large number of our subjects, who make use of Negro slaves for the cultivation of the land. We have judged that it belongs to our authority and justice for the preservation of this colony to establish a law and certain regulations for the maintenance of the discipline of the Catholic, Apostolic, and Roman Church and to ordain what concerns the situation and quality of the slaves in the aforesaid islands....For these causes and others moving to Us on the advice of our Council, and with our own certain knowledge, full power, and royal authority, we have spoken, stated, and ordained, let us say, we decree and ordain, We wish and there pleases us what follows:

ARTICLE FIRST

The edict of the late King Louis XIII, of glorious memory, of the 23 April 1615, will be executed in our province and colony of Louisiana; this being done, we enjoin the Directors General of the aforesaid Company, and all our officials to expel from the aforesaid country all of the Jews who may have established their residence there, as they are the declared enemy of the Christian name, We command them to leave within three months, counting from the day of the publication of this present [decree] under penalty of the confiscation of their person and property.

II.

All the slaves who are found in our aforesaid province, shall be instructed and baptized in the Catholic, Apostolic, and Roman Religion: we order the inhabitants who shall purchase newly arrived blacks to have them instructed and baptized within a suitable time under penalty of an arbitrary fine. We enjoin the Directors General of the aforesaid Company and all officials to enforce this exactly.

III.

We forbid all exercise of another religion than that of the Catholic, Apostolic, and Roman; We wish that those contravening [this order] be punished as rebels and disobedient to our commandments: We forbid all assemblies for this purpose, which [assemblies] We declare them as unlawful and seditious conventicles, subject to the same penalty, which will take place against the slaveowners who shall permit them or permit their slaves in this regard.

IV.

No commanders shall be in charge of the blacks who does not profess the Catholic, Apostolic, and Roman religion under penalty of confiscation of the aforesaid blacks against the masters who had charge of them and of arbitrary punishment against the owners who shall have accepted the aforesaid charge.

V.

We enjoin on all of our subjects of whatever quality and condition they are to observe regularly Sundays and Feastdays; We forbid them to work their slaves nor to have their slaves forced to work on the farms or any other tasks on the aforesaid days from midnight of the day to the midnight of the next day under penalty of a fine and of arbitrary punishment against the slaveholders and the confiscation of the slaves who shall be caught in the work by our officials. They shall nevertheless be able to send their slaves to market.

VI.

We forbid our white subjects of one and the other sex to contract a marriage with the blacks under pain of punishment and arbitrary fine; and to all pastors, priests, or missionaries, both secular and religious and even to chaplains of vessels to marry them. We also forbid our white subjects and even freed blacks and those born free to live in concubinage with slaves. We wish that those who shall have had one or several children from such a union together with the master who shall have permitted it shall each be condemned to a fine of three hundred *livres.* And if they are the owner of the slave by whom they shall have had the aforesaid children, we wish that beside the fine they shall be deprived both of the slave as well as the children, and that they [the slave and the children] shall be adjudged to the hospital of the place without ever being able to be freed. We do not intend, however, that the present article shall take effect when a black man, freedman or born free, who is not married during the concubinage with his slave, shall marry the same slave within the prescribed forms by the Church, the slave shall be set free by this means and the children shall be rendered free and legitimate.

VII.

The solemnities prescribed by the Ordinance of Blois and by the declaration of 1639 for marriages, shall be observed both in regard to free persons as well as slaves; without nevertheless that the consent of the father and mother of the slave shall be necessary, but that of the slaveowner only.

VIII.

We expressly forbid the pastors to proceed with the marriage of slaves if they do not make evident the consent of their masters: We forbid also that masters use any constraint on their slaves to marry against their will.

IX.

The children who will be born from the marriage of slaves shall be slaves and they will belong to the masters of the female slaves and not to those of their husbands if the husbands and wives have different owners.

X.

We will that if the slave husband has married a free woman that both the male and female children follow the condition of their mother and that they be free as she is despite the servitude of their father; and that if the father is free and the mother a slave, the children shall likewise be slaves.

XI.

The slaveowners shall be bound to bury their baptized slaves in consecrated ground in cemeteries destined for that purpose; and in regard to those who shall die without having received baptism, they shall be interred during the night in some field adjacent to the place where they shall have died.

XII.

We forbid to slaves to carry any offensive arms not even a heavy stick under the penalty of a flogging and the confiscation of the arms for the profit of the one who shall have taken possession of it with the sole exception of those who shall have been sent out to hunt on behalf of their owners and who shall carry papers to that effect or other recognized marks of identity.

XIII.

We likewise forbid slaves belonging to different owners to come together by day or by night under pretext of weddings or other things whether at the home of one of their masters or others, and still less on major roads or remote places under pain of corporal punishment which cannot be less than a whipping and the branding with the *fleur de Lys;* and in the case of frequent recidivists and other aggravating circumstances can be punishable by death, which we leave up to the discretion of the judges: we enjoin all of our subjects to pursue those violating [this ordinance] and arrest them and put them in prison even if they may not be officers nor there be any warrant against them....

XXVII.

The slave who will have struck his owner, his mistress, the husband of his mistress, or their children with bruising and the spilling of blood, or [a blow] to the face, will be punishable by death....

XXXII.

The fugitive slave who will have been in flight for a month, counting from the day that his owner will have denounced him to the judge shall have his ears cropped and shall be branded with a *fleur de Lys* on one shoulder; and if he will try again for another month, likewise counting from the day of denunciation, he shall have the tendon of the leg cut and be branded on the other shoulder; and on a third attempt, he shall be punished with death....

XXXIV.

Freedmen or free blacks who will have given shelter in their homes to fugitive slaves shall be condemned physically toward the owner with a fine of thirty *livres* for each day of shelter; and other free persons who shall have given like shelter [shall be fined] ten *livres* for each day of shelter; and in case of default by the aforesaid freedmen or free blacks in being able to pay the fine, they shall be reduced to the condition of slaves and sold and if the price of the sale is greater than the fine, the surplus shall go the hospital....

XLIII.

We wish nonetheless that the husband, his wife, and their young children who have not reached puberty, shall not be taken into possession for debt and be sold into debt if they shall all be property of the same owner; We declare null such legal procedures and separate sales that could be made....[1]

L.

Slave owners who are twenty-five years or older shall be able to free their slaves by any legal act *inter vivos*[2] or by will and testament: however, as there may be found slave owners mercenary enough to place the freedom of their slaves at a price which might bring the aforesaid slaves to theft or robbery, we forbid all persons of whatever quality and condition they may be to free their slaves without having obtained permission by an act of our said Superior Council; which permission will be granted without cost when the motives which shall have been given by the owners will appear legitimate. We wish that the manumissions which shall be made in the future without these permissions shall be null and that the freed persons shall not be able

---

1. The article forbids the separation and individual sale of members of a slave family that has been seized by creditors of a deceased owner for the payment of debts. The article forbids the sale of children under fourteen years of age away from their parents. [Ed.]

2. Both contracting parties are alive. [Ed.]

to profit there from nor be reputed as free. We order, on the contrary, that they shall be held, considered, and reputed as slaves, that the owners shall be deprived of them, and that they shall be confiscated for the Company of the Indies.

LI.

We wish, nevertheless, that the slaves who shall have been named by their owners as Guardians of their children shall be held and reputed as We hold and consider them for freed persons....

LIII.

We command to all freed persons to have a singular respect for their former masters, to their widows, and to their children; in such a way that an injury that they shall have perpetrated, shall be punished more grievously than if it had been done by another person. The directors, however, shall dismiss against them any other charges, services, and legal rights that their former masters would claim as patrons either on their persons or their goods and property.

LIV.

We grant to the freed persons the same rights, privileges, and immunities which freeborn persons enjoy. We wish that the merit of acquired liberty might produce in them both for their persons as for their property the same effects that the happiness of natural liberty causes for our other subjects....

So that the aforesaid things might remain firm and stable in the time to come, We have placed our seal.

Given at Versailles in the month of March, in the year of grace one thousand seven hundred and twenty four, and of our reign the nineteenth. *Signed* LOUIS *Added further down* the King....

Le Code Noir ou Edit du Roy (Paris: De l'Imprimerie Royale, 1727); Tulane University, Howard Tilton Memorial Library, Rare Books, with permission

4. The Ursuline Nuns Limit Their Instruction of Girls of Color, 1797

The Ursuline nuns arrived in New Orleans in 1727, nine years after the foundation of New Orleans. From the beginning they brought a certain civility and respectability to the port city of easy morals and casual laws. The

nuns opened a school for young ladies and a hospital. They not only taught young women who were white but also Native American and black women. In 1797, the nuns were asked to teach mulatto women. The question was posed to the community council. The following comments translated from the Spanish original were placed in the community council minutes.

In the City of New Orleans, the 31st of October, 1797, Sister Theresa of St. Xavier Farjon, Superior of this Monastery of St. Ursula, after the chapter of faults, proposed to the Community the following: whether they were willing to admit to the day school for instruction and within the convent as half boarders the mulattoes who were applying for this arrangement. They answered unanimously that they would not, except the legitimate daughters whose parents were white father and quadroon mother as they have been received until now. The others would be received only if they were separated from the others, so that they might be instructed in the Christian Religion. So that [it] might be known in the future, I record it in this book of my office on the 14th of November of the year above mentioned. I will sign it after the Rev. Mother Superior, who must sign it.

Sister Theresa of St. Xavier Farjon, Supr.

Sister Antonia of St. Monica Ramos, Secretary

"Community Council Minutes," October 31, 1797, Archives of the Ursuline Nuns in New Orleans. Translated by Sister Jane Frances Heaney, with permission.

Part 2

THE PRE–CIVIL WAR PERIOD

One of the oldest black Catholic communities before the Civil War was found in Baltimore, Maryland, a border city where there were many free blacks as well as slaves. Baltimore was the capital of a state where there were numerous Catholics. In fact, the city was named for Cecil Calvert, the second Lord Baltimore, a Roman Catholic, who had received Maryland as a proprietary colony in 1634, where Roman Catholics enjoyed religious liberty. In 1785, John Carroll, the leading Roman Catholic priest and soon to be named first bishop in the newly formed United States, wrote that there were three thousand Catholics of African origin in the state. In 1793, this number was increased with the arrival of a boatload of some six hundred blacks from the former French colony of St-Domingue (now Haiti). They were fugitives from a country then in revolution. In 1789, Carroll was named the first bishop in the United States and Baltimore was named the first See.

The Sulpicians arrived in the United States from France in 1791. They not only opened a seminary for the training of priests in Baltimore; they also ministered to the faithful in many different ways. In the Sulpician Archives in Baltimore, there is a small leather-bound notebook of fifty-five pages entitled *Records of Confraternities.*[1] In this notebook are handwritten lists of names for four confraternities: Our Lady of Mount Carmel; Our Lady, Help of Christians; Our Lady of the Rosary; and the Confraternity of the Sacred Heart.[2] Membership in these confraternities was completely voluntary. Those who were enrolled in the confraternities agreed to perform certain acts of piety, which often meant the recitation of certain prayers, communion on specific days, and the wearing of some medal or a cloth scapular. Membership in the confraternity often indicated that the individual member sought to obtain certain spiritual benefits, provided that he or she was faithful to the duties of a confraternity member.

---

1. Records of Confraternities, RG 1, Box 17, Sulpician Archives, Baltimore.
2. The notebook also contains the ritual for the conferral of the scapular and a list of the 1850 census for St. Mary's Seminary and College.

The Confraternity of Our Lady of Mount Carmel was under the direction of Bishop Carroll. It began in Maryland in 1796. The lists contained the names of the members and the date of their enrollment in the confraternity between that date and 1858. The membership listed the names of men and women, clergy and laity, whites and blacks, slaves and free. With an average of twenty-five names per page over a space of fifty-five pages, there were, it seems, over a thousand names in a span of sixty years. Of those names over a third were identified as black or mulattoes, slaves and free persons. Persons of African descent were found in the listing of some of the other confraternities as well, but the number was not as great as that of Our Lady of Mount Carmel. Perhaps one might draw the conclusion that black Catholics in antebellum Maryland were at the same level of piety and spirituality as the white Catholic laity. The following excerpt presents the names found on the first three pages of the book. The entries were made in French. The letters N and M stood for Negro (*Nègre*) and Mulatto (*Mulâtre*), respectively.

5. The Devotional Life of Blacks in the Confraternity of Mount Carmel, 1796

Register

The names of the persons who have been received into the Confraternity of Our Lady of Mount Carmel established in Baltimore under the direction and by the authority of Most Reverend Bishop Carroll according to the power that he has received from the Superior General of the Order of Carmelites in the month of January 1796.

1796

January 7.	has been received Marie LaCombe.
	Fortunée, black woman of M. Dennis.[1]
	Sophia, a free Mulatto woman
	Veronique, black woman of Madame La Lannée
Sept. 11.	Alzire, a free Mulatto woman
	Lucile, a free Mulatto woman
October 2.	Jean Batiste, a black man of Mr. Gearity
	Marie Theophile, a Mulatto woman of Mr. Clery
	Emilie, a Mulatto woman of M. Autriessean

1. Fortunée is indicated as the slave of Mr. Dennis. The words *Negresse, Nègre* have been translated as "black woman" and "black man." Often the text has simply N or M. One who was designated as the "person of" indicated a slave. [Ed.]

1797

February 11.	Elizabeth Brigitt Kempe
February 16.	Demetrius Augustin Gallitzin, alias Smith[2]
February 19.	Alzire, a black woman of Madame Ponce[3]
February 26.	Modeste, a black woman of Madame Assailly
April 5.	Marie Therese Marsan
	Louise Francoise Marsan
	Jeanne Magdalaine Marsan
	Clarisse Barrere
May 3.	Marie Therese, widow Marsan
June 15.	Marie Elizabeth Laly Lambert
July 2.	Jean-Pierre, a black slave of Madame Desmangler
July 16.	Adelaide La Clerc
July 23.	Marie Michel, Asnotte [?], a black slave, of Madame Conti
August 15.	Magdelaine, a Mulatto slave of Madame Lacombe
	Jane Mary Fariar
September 20.	Garret Burns
October 2.	Marie Francoise Antoinette Heloïse
December 8.	Lucile Fortunée, a black woman
	Lucile Maria Magdalaine; a Mulatto woman…

1815.

January 15.	John and Sarah Parsons
May 7.	Mary Griffith
June 18.	Pierre Cupidon, a black man
	Louis Cesar, a black man
	Jean Francois, a black man
	Marie Jeanne [?], a black woman
	Marie Louise Sophie, a black woman
July 16.	Anne Francoise LaRue
	Marie Louise, a black woman
	Louise Elizabeth, a black woman
	Louis Cezar, a black man

---

2. Demetrius Gallitzin (1770–1840) was born in Holland, the son of a Russian prince, who migrated to the United States and became the first priest (1795) to have received all of his seminary training in the United States. [Ed.]

3. The name is uncertain. [Ed.]

Nicholas Charles, a black man

Marie Catherine

Marie Zamire, black slave of M. Servari

17.   Louis Le Roy

Marie Claire Clairvause, a black woman

Marie Magd. Isaurine Balas, a Mulatto woman

Clarisse, Elisabeth Lange

Catharine McGowen[4]

Records of Confraternities, RG1, Box 17 "Confraternity of Our Lady of Mount Carmel," 1796, 1797, 1815, Sulpician Archives, Baltimore, with permission.

6. Portrait of a Saintly Slave, 1806

Many Maryland Catholics began to move to the frontier territory of Kentucky at the end of the eighteenth century. They came with their slaves. Most of these slaves were Catholics like their owners. The following is a description of a slave named Harry, who was the slave of Stephen Badin, a priest born in France in 1768, who came to the United States in 1792, became the first man ordained a priest in the United States in 1793, and arrived in Kentucky as missionary in the same year. Martin J. Spalding, the future bishop of Louisville and archbishop of Baltimore, wrote an account of the early history of Catholicism in Kentucky. Much of it was devoted to the reminiscences of the first Catholic priest in Kentucky, Stephen Badin. The following is the description of a very devout slave who became the slave of Father Badin toward the end of his life. The text is important because it portrays the piety of a black man who inspired his contemporaries. At the same time, the language and the sentiments attributed to this holy man as described by Badin himself reveal the inability of white people of that time to appreciate the dignity of a slave and the basic equality of all people before God.

Among the models of piety, which abounded during the time of which we are treating, we cannot omit to say a few words concerning one who was as eminent for his virtue, as he was lowly in condition. The name of the truly pious and exemplary negro servant, commonly called "Uncle Harry," is familiar to most of the older Catholic settlers of Kentucky. He was truly

---

4. Marie Balas, who is described with an M, and Elizabeth Lange, without any letter, were both foundresses of the Oblate Sisters of Providence founded with the approval of Archbishop Whitfield in 1829. They were the first successful black religious congregation of women. The name of Catharine McGowen was crossed out. The fact that Elizabeth Lange was not designated as a mulatto woman probably indicates that some blacks were not identified as such. [Ed.]

a model of every Christian virtue. On the death of his master, he became the property of infant heirs. An old and faithful family servant, he was left by the executor to his own choice in the selection of his employment. He determined to go to the saltlicks, thinking that there he could earn most by his labour, for the benefit of the young heirs. Before departing, however, he determined to consult M. Badin on the step he was about to take. His pastor endeavoured at first to dissuade him from his purpose, representing the hardships he would there have to undergo, the distance from church, and the danger to which his salvation would be exposed.

"Uncle Harry" replied to this last reason, with the utmost simplicity of faith: "that God would protect him from danger, and that the Blessed Virgin would take care of him." M. Badin yielded. At the licks, "Uncle Harry" was a model of piety for all. When any one of his fellow-servants was sick, he was always called for; and on these occasions, he did every thing in his power to console and instruct the sick person, by the bedside of whom he was wont to recite his beads, and to say all the prayers he knew. Sometimes afterwards he was publicly sold, and purchased by a man who was not a Catholic. He obtained permission to see M. Badin, whom he induced to purchase him promising that his labour should more than indemnify him for whatever expense he might incur. A year or two later, M. Badin visited him while he was labouring in the field: he appeared sad and dejected, and on being asked the reason, he replied, that he was fearful that he might die before he could repay his kind master what he had expended. M. Badin comforted him, and the good negro again put on a cheerful countenance.

He said prayers morning and night, with the other servants, who had great respect for his virtue. He gave them the most comfortable beds, and often spent the night in prayer, taking but a brief repose, on the hard floor. In the church, he always knelt as immoveable as a statue; and was often there for hours before the rest of the congregation. His whole life, in fact, seemed to be one continual prayer: and he died, as he had lived, praying. He expired without a struggle. One morning he was found dead, sitting upright on a stool, his hands clasped in prayer, holding his beads, and his countenance irradiated with a sweet smile. His death occurred in 1806.[1]

M. J. Spalding, *Sketches of the Early Catholic Missions of Kentucky; From Their Commencement in 1787, to the Jubilee of 1826–7* (Louisville: B. J. Webb and Brother, 1844), 116–17.

---

1. Those who were acquainted with "Uncle Harry" will know that the picture above drawn of him is not too highly coloured. Virtue is admirable, wherever found, and God often chooses the humblest individuals as His most special favourites. [Footnote in original.]

7. Petition of the Catholic People of Color in Philadelphia, 1817

This petition from the black Catholic community in Philadelphia is one of the earliest documents we have that indicates the presence of a black Catholic community in pre–Civil War Philadelphia. The six witnesses have English names and presumably are representative of a larger community. This petition was made to the trustees of St. Mary's Church in a time when the running of the parish church was often in the charge of lay trustees.

At a meeting of the Board of Trustees of St. Mary's Church Philadelphia, held November 15th 1817 the following Petition from "The Catholic People of Color residing in Philadelphia," was presented.

The Petition of the Catholic People of Color residing in Philadelphia humbly showeth:

That your petitioners are destitute of the means to give their children a Catholic education: That the different Sectarians are seeking and encouraging us to send them that they may instruct them, but if we do they instruct them their way. That our children are destitute of the means to acquire the knowledge of our religion and the duties whereby they might be able to repel the incessant attacks made on them by a set of beings who can quote the Scriptures with every phrase in order to seduce the ignorant. We tremble for the fate of our children some of whom have been already seduced from our religion. Therefore we sincerely hope that your charitable Board will take them under your protecting wing as you have taken the poor of your own colour and to have ours also instructed in a common English education and to appoint a teacher who will be careful above all things to cause them to know their catechism and have them say their morning and evening prayers, and we shall ever pray.

Joseph Burns,	John Diamond,	John Scott,
Thos. Keen,	Simon Hadock,	John Carroll.

The petition was referred to a Committee. It reported that in consequence of the heavy debt — the support of the St. Joseph's Society and the poor of the congregation that nothing could be done until Summer. The records of the Trustees contain nothing to show that in "Summer" the matter of the Petition received any attention.

Courtesy of the Sulpician Archives, Baltimore; the document was published in the *American Catholic Historical Researches* 7 (1890): 185.

8. The Clandestine Marriages of Slaves, 1839

Slaves were not permitted to marry unless they had the permission of their owners. The clergy were unable to officiate at their marriages unless this permission had been obtained. Freedom to marry, however, is a right based upon the Natural Law. Just as no slave master could interfere with a slave's worship of God, so the owner could not control the marriage of one's slaves. These principles, of course, were often not respected. In the light of the Church's respect for the Natural Law, Pope Leo XII (1823–29) published a decree stating that as long as the marriages of slaves were not free, the clandestine marriages of slaves were to be considered valid. The priest must keep a record of these marriages, which were to be placed in a special place in the diocesan archives.[1] Théodore de Theux, S.J., was stationed at Grand Côteau, where the Jesuits operated a college and ministered to the laity in the area. It is not known whether Father de Theux was aware of the decree of Pope Leo XII issued in 1828. Nor is it known whether the letter to Bishop Blanc was answered. The letter is important, however, because it is one of the few documents that provide us with a notion of how the question of slaves' marriages were treated from a pastoral point of view.

Théodore de Theux, S.J., to Antoine Blanc.
Grand Côteau, 3 June 1839.

Monseigneur,

I imagine that Your Grace on returning from your apostolic tour and, I hope, after having accomplished much good is in good health. The Vicar General having been good enough to promise me to present to you this humble request of Father Paillason and of your servant, I leave all in this way in good hands....

In regard to the marriage of slaves, *those in servitude to masters*. Here is what appears to us to be able to be done; and would His Grace be so good to tell us what he thinks. "We shall say in confession to one of the parties, in order to marry, mutually take one another (after having well explained the nature of the contract). Thereupon suggest to some slaves on the same farm to have the intention to frequent the sacraments."

As far as we are concerned, if anyone speaks to us about it, we shall respond: "It must be supposed that these people have been married naturally, as they could not do otherwise, their marriage must be considered valid."

We commend ourselves very humbly as well as the flock which has been entrusted to us to the prayers of your Grace.

I have the honor to be with the most profound respect

> Monseigneur, the most humble and obedient servant of
> Your Grace,
> T. de Theux, S.J. Min.

---

1. See *Lettere e Decreti della S. Congregazione e Biglietti di Mons. Segretario, 1828,* vol. 309, fol. 758r–758v, Congregation of the Propaganda Archives, University of Notre Dame. See also Cyprian Davis, *The History of Black Catholics in the United States* (New York: Crossroad, 1991), 274 n.54.

P.S. In order to more surely prevent a scandal, can we not say openly — and that from the pulpit — that these people of color, as far as one of the parties are slaves, who cannot marry before the Church, can do so naturally after having consulted their confessor to do so; and to frequent thereafter the Sacraments? Monseigneur, would you kindly reply clearly in regard to all of this.

v-4-h, Théodore de Theux, S.J., to Antoine Blanc, Grand Côteau, June 3, 1839, Archives of the University of Notre Dame, with permission.

9. A Catholic Mutual Benefit Society, 1843

As early as the 1780s, blacks began to form mutual benevolent societies where aid and support could be assured for each member. In recent years it has become clear that black Catholics also formed mutual benevolent societies. One of the earliest of these societies is the Society of the Holy Family established in the cathedral parish of Baltimore. A record of the weekly Sunday evening meetings was kept by the spiritual director, Father John F. Hickey, a Sulpician, who was curate at the cathedral parish. The society met from the end of 1843 to the fall of 1845. This record is in a notebook of over seventy pages in the Sulpician Archives in Baltimore. From all evidence the society continued its existence at the chapel of the Oblate Sisters of Providence when they were unable to meet longer in the rooms they had used in Calvert Hall. The membership listed almost two hundred persons. Possibly some of them were slaves. The following passages are excerpts from the record kept by Father Hickey.

Journal of the commencement and of the proceedings of the Society of Coloured people; with the approbation of the Most Rev. Archbishop Samuel[1] and of the Rector of the Cathedral, Rev. H. B. Coskery.

1st Session

The first meeting was held in the basement of Calvert Hall on the 1st Sunday of Advent, 3rd of December 1843. The 1st meeting was numerous amounting to about 150 or 200 — females and males — John F. Hickey, assistant at the cathedral, acted as Director — during that meeting, which began by invocation of the Holy Ghost, an instruction on the great truths of Religion was given; the principal object of the meeting explained — viz. the affording of the colored people an opportunity of attending more particularly to their salvation and spiritual concerns — 2°. the adopting of such

---

1. Samuel Eccleston (1801–51) was archbishop of Baltimore from 1834 to 1851.

regulation, as may tend to render the society useful. 3°. The selecting of a name, which was to be given by the majority of votes, and of the officers to be employed in the society. etc. etc. — After speaking himself the director requested any gentleman or lady to give expression to his or her ideas relative to the matter before the society — after singing, praying, and making a collection of 90 cents the society adjourned.

2nd Session

10th December 1843. The 2nd Sunday of Advent the 2nd meeting of the Society took place at 7 o'clock the same as the first meeting and at the same place. *Dirigente J.F.H.* [Under the direction of John F. Hickey] after prayers and instruction the votes were taken for the naming of the society. Accordingly 75 votes were given for the name of "The Holy Family" and 70 votes for the name of "the St. Benedict's Society."[2] — of course it was then and there called the *Holy Family.* — after a few remarks made by two or three members — both useful and proper — after singing some hymns as at the 1st meeting — saying prayers and collecting $3.46. The meeting adjourned. — ...

11th Session

The 11th meeting of the Society of the Holy Family was held in Calvert Hall on 18th February 1844 — It began 7 o'clock. First by singing a hymn, "Come Holy Ghost" etc. Their beads. 1st decade, on knees. 2nd two standing. 3rd decade kneeling. Then instruction drawn from the Gospel, 1/2 or 3/4 of an hour. Then another short hymn, during which the collection was made, then remarks, more peculiarly relating to the temporal and spiritual concerns of the society, exhorting them to preach to others by good example and to admonish each other mildly and charitably, etc. Then asking at the same time if the President or any officer or member had any remarks to make. Afterwards a hymn and night prayers. Some paid in their monthly subscription and gave something towards the cathedral fund. I was introduced to a woman who wished to become a practical Catholick [*sic*] from having been only desirous of instruction in a half kind of a way. By 9 o'clock all had left.

---

2. This St. Benedict was St. Benedict the Moor (c. 1526–89), ex-slave born in Sicily of African parents. A Franciscan friar, he was canonized by Pope Pius VII in 1807. Among black Catholics there developed great devotion to him.

25th Session, 16th June

The 25th meeting of the Society of the Holy Family was held this evening at Calvert Hall. Meeting large...singing very well. Jane came out with something about the rock of Peter. Council did not meet on Tuesday last, invited for tomorrow evening.[3]

RGG42 Box 2, Sulpician Archives, Baltimore, with permission.

10. Memoir of Pierre Toussaint, Born a Slave in Santo Domingo, 1854

Pierre Toussaint (1766–1853) was born a slave in Haiti, or as it was known at the time, St-Domingue. In this French colony, the harsh working conditions resulted in a very high mortality rate. As a result the trade in slaves from Africa was extremely high. Besides the African population, there was a significant population of mulattoes, most of whom were free, and many of whom were educated in France.

Pierre Toussaint had been born on the plantation of the Bérard family. He was not of mixed parentage, but his mother and grandmother held important positions among the slaves on the plantation. Pierre himself grew up as a domestic in the household of Jean Bérard. He was given an opportunity to learn to read and write and was reared in the Catholic religion. In 1787, Pierre Toussaint accompanied his owner, Jean Bérard, to New York City along with Madame Bérard, his sister and his aunt. Monsieur Bérard returned to Haiti to liquidate his holdings but was caught in the troubles. He himself was struck down by pleurisy and died, leaving his widow with worthless stocks and bonds, on the verge of poverty.

Like many urban slaves Toussaint acquired a trade. He was apprenticed as a hairdresser. Because of the demand for fashionable hair styles, Toussaint soon developed a thriving business among the well-to-do ladies of New York City society. Madame Bérard was supported totally by the kindness of her slave, Toussaint. In 1807 he was manumitted shortly before her death.

Toussaint lived a life of singular piety, extraordinary magnanimity, and constant service to others. He died in 1853, universally acclaimed as a saint. The life of the Venerable Pierre Toussaint was published the year after his death by one of those who had known him as a hairdresser and a friend. Hence, much of the information came from an eyewitness.

---

3. Besides the weekly Sunday meetings, there was a meeting during certain weeks of the officers of the society who dealt with certain issues as regulations and procedure. Jane Thompson often broke out in spontaneous prayer.

The period in Toussaint's life which occurred from the time of Euphemia's[1] death for a succession of years seems to have been an uncommonly tranquil one. His union with Juliette was happy. She was the daughter of a respectable woman named Claudine Gaston, who came to this country as a nurse, as has been before mentioned, with a French family, by whom she was much beloved. She was a judicious and an affectionate wife, by her neatness and order making his house pleasant to him, and taking a more than equal share in the labors of the family.

Every man must value the respect of his wife, and Toussaint could not but be gratified with the evident delight Juliette received from the attentions paid him. When her friends congratulated her on having such a good husband, her frank, happy smile, displaying rows of white teeth, gave a full assent to their commendations.

Toussaint said of himself, that he possessed a quick temper, that he was born with it, and was obliged to bear it about with him. We doubt not that it was true, because he had a lively sensibility to every thing; yet to those who knew his self-command and forbearance, this trait made him the more interesting. One of his intimate friends, in alluding to his confessions and penitence on the subject, said: "I never heard him speak ill of any one if he could say no good, he was silent. Even those who were ungrateful to him met with no angry rebuke; it seemed to be his object to forget all injuries."

Toussaint had a quick sense of the ridiculous, and like most of his race, when he was young, was an excellent mimic; as he grew older he relinquished this power, so amusing to others, as a dangerous one. He played on the violin for small dancing parties at one time, and taught one or two boys to play on this instrument, saying, if they did not derive profit from it, it would at least be an innocent amusement.

One of the methods in which Toussaint did essential good was by bringing up colored boys one after another, sending them to school, and, after they were old enough, teaching them some useful business. In all these plans of charity Juliette united.

> Hannah Farnham Sawyer Lee, *Memoir of Pierre Toussaint, Born a Slave in St. Domingo* (Boston: Crosby, Nichols, 1854), 80–82.

11. Two Letters by Pierre Toussaint, 1839

Pierre Toussaint bought the freedom of Juliette, whom he married. She was twenty years younger than he. Haitian, like him, Juliette had relatives in Baltimore and connections with the Oblate Sisters of Providence. In 1839, she

---

1. Euphemia was Toussaint's sister's daughter, whom he raised. She died at the age of fourteen.

The Venerable Pierre Toussaint (1766–1853). Image reprinted from Arthur and Elizabeth Sheehan, *A Citizen of Old New York* (New York: P. J. Kenedy & Sons, 1955).

visited her friends in Baltimore. This was seemingly one of the few times that Pierre and his wife were separated. He wrote her twice. He missed her terribly, but he did not want to curtail her enjoyment. Most letters from him and to him were written in French. Toussaint's handwriting was that of a man who never learned to write well. His warm affection for his wife is apparent despite the stilted language. He addressed his wife with the formal second person "vous." He used no paragraphs.[1]

---

1. All the documents relating to Pierre Toussaint, including the biography by Hannah Sawyer Lee, are found in the New York Public Library, Manuscript and Rare Books Section, Pierre Toussaint Papers. [Ed.]

New York, July 8, 1833

Dear Juliette,

I have just received your letter dated the 6th. I feel much better that your illness has left you at rest. Thank God, I am still in good health. Your mother is also well, and all of your friends ask me if I have any news from you. I always tell them that Madame Toussaint is doing very well. Thank God. And that she is having a good time with her friends of Baltimore. I am indeed indebted to the ladies and gentlemen that they have welcomed you so well. Speak to them many words of friendship [on my part] especially to Madame Monpensier. Tell her that I ask her not to spoil you too much. At the same time I charge you to follow her example. . . . Francis and Monsieur _____[2] send you many respectful greetings. Madame Schuyler sends greeting; Mr George was astonished that I have allowed you to go all alone, I told him that my own business must pass always before all else and that my wife is with good company and that I hope that she is very happy and that is all my consolation. Tell me if you have heard some sermons in French. I dined yesterday with Madame Custine. Josephine and her mother wish you many good things. She asks you to give her greetings to all the ladies. Madame Michel and her mother send you greetings. The ladies Jeannerose do not forget you. They send their compliments to Madame Noël without forgetting Madame Monpensier. Cabrisse has not forgotten anyone. *Adieu,* my dear friend. I am sending you a thousand embraces. I am yours in Christ,

P. Toussaint

New York, July 13, 1833

My dearest Wife,

I have just received your letter, dated the 11th. You see that I am answering at once. Thanks to God that all is going well here. I wish to see you; but with such a wish, I desire that you stay as long a time as you wish. For I love my wife for herself; not for me.

If you are enjoying yourself in Baltimore, I plead with you to remain several days more with your good friends; and I in turn thank them for the welcome that they have given you. Give them my greetings, especially to Fanny. Say to her that I beg her not to give you too much bad example. I know that she is so devout and so full of mischief. I wish that you take with you a little of her devotion and a little of her mischief. Your mother and your brother are well. They send their greeting. Monsieur and Madame Gentil and Theodore often speak of you. The ladies _____ send you a

---

2. Name is illegible. [Ed.]

thousand messages. Monsieur and Madame Villagraves (?)[3] send their greetings. Mademoiselle Justine and Mimi do not forget you. Félicie and Ma
her mother speak of you. The ladies Plaitte send greetings. You have said
nothing in regard to Monsieur Dan.... Say to him please thousands and
thousands greetings on my part. How go things with the son of Justine
Cabrise. Do not forget the *Bonne Presse* (?) and Madame with greeting (?).
Madame Vail (?) asks you to not forget the *Manuel du Chrétien.* Madame
Salle [*sic*] sends greetings. Josephine often speaks of you. She begs you to
give a thousand greetings to Madame Noël and to Madame Monpensier.
The ladies Plaitte beg you not to forget to greet for them the two ladies
Madame Noël and Fanny — the ladies Mies, the ladies Binsse, the ladies
Varet — all say to you many greetings. *Adieu.* I embrace you with all my
heart. *Adieu,* dear friend. I am your faithful.

Pierre Toussaint

12. George Paddington, Black Priest from Ireland, Missionary in Haiti, Friend of Pierre Toussaint, 1836

George Paddington was a black priest about whom we know very little.
Most of the information about him comes from the letters that he sent to
Pierre Toussaint. The Paddingtons were a black family located in Dublin.
There seems to have been an almost nonexistent population of blacks in
nineteenth-century Dublin. The family members were acrobats. It is not
clear how Paddington came to know the Toussaints. The letters make it
clear that he felt very close to them. His letters confirm the fact that
Bishop England of Charleston ordained him. The letters reveal that Padding-
ton saw the United States as a "cursed land of slavery." After learning
French and being assigned to pastoral work, he left Haiti and went to
Rome for more study. Did he return to Haiti? It is not certain. As one of
the first priests of African descent outside of Africa, these letters supply
some meager information about a very important historical figure in black
Catholic history.

Port-au-Prince, 30 March 1836

My Dear Friends,

I take, with pleasure, a few moments afforded me of writing a few lines to
you. You will be pleased to hear that the climate agrees with me at present
extremely well and that I am enjoying the best health. I hope in God you
enjoy the same. It would have given me much pleasure to see you again in
New York but the President and the Bishop did not wish me to leave the
country in order to finish my studies in Rome nor [*sic*] in France. I was

---

3. The question marks indicate that the name is illegible. [Ed.]

ordained Subdeacon on the 13 inst. and immediately after my ordination the President sent to tell the Bishop that he appointed [me] as Professor in the new College at La Coupe, eight miles from the city [word scratched out] the Bishop returned to Charleston last week and I remain here probabbly [*sic*] for the rest of my life. The Bishop is to return in October next and three other Bishops and many Clergymen are to be appointed. When the Bishop returns everything will be regulated and I believe in another year I am to receive other orders for I will know something of the french language in that time. The country and the people are, I think, the finest and the kindest ever met with; but I have no doubt but that if faithfully served by good ministers of religion and other instructors, they would become the best people I know of. As I have no more time to be particular at present, I must content myself with what I have said, but I promise to serve you a long letter the next opportunity I can lay hold on.

Geo. I. Paddington

Mr. and Mrs. Toussaint

I expect you will write to me at every opportunity and Direct for me at the Seminary La Coupe to the Care of Rev. Mr. Cervalto's (?) Presbetery [*sic*]. Port-au-Prince.

Pétionville Seminary, 25 July 1836.

My dear Friends Toussaint,

I received your affectionate (letter) of 15 May from the hands of my friend Guercin and I would have answered it long before but could not find an opportunity before this. I feel really obliged and return a thousand to you and my Dear friend Madame Toussaint for your kind solicitude about my health which, thank God, still continues excellent and by care I (think) the climate will always agree with me. I know you will be delighted to hear that I was ordained Priest on 21 day of last May by the Rt. Rev^d, D^r. England, in the Church of Port-au-Prince. I said my first Mass on Trinity Sunday and [be] you rest assured that I did not, nor can I ever, forget my friends whenever I celebrate the divine mysteries among whom I shall always consider you and Madame Toussaint as particularly dear to me. I now celebrate mass every day in the Church at Petionville where I remain at present 'till the Bishop returns from Rome. I celebrate one mass for you and Madame T. about ten days ago — you may be sure that I was extremely sorry to hear of the bad health of my Dear Friend D^r. Power but am glad that he now (I hope) quite recovered, for he wrote me two kind letters in which he mentions his gradual recovery. I was sorry to hear that the roof of your favorite church (St. Peter's) had fallen in, thank God that neither you nor any of the congregation were in it at the time. And I hope that the people will come forward with piety and liberality to build a new and more elegant temple to God in the same place and that quickly — I gave your good wishes to Mr Constantine Boyer and family. His son had a slight fever last week but is getting better. His family send you their best respects. I never saw M. Benoit since I came to Port-au-Prince. I was told that he and his family left this Country about three weeks ago and returned to live again in New York or in some other part of that cursed land of Slavery, N. America. I have sent an "Imitation of Christ" to Madame Toussaint as a small tribute hoping it may be acceptable to so good a Friend. I would also send you something as a memorial of my friendship for you but as yet I have seen nothing that I think would please you, but I won't forget some little matter for you as soon as I can meet it. I pray you to make my best respects to all friends in New York who may enquire about me — I hope you will write to me every time you have an opportunity, and I won't fail to answer your letters should I get them. And now my dear friend, sending you and your kind lady my best wishes and begging the continuance of your prayers for me, I beg of God to bless you both, and me.

Sincerely your friend
Geo. I. Paddington.

New York Public Library, Manuscript Department, Papers of Pierre Toussaint, microfilm, with permission.

13. A Black Woman's Letter to Pope Pius IX, 1853

In a long handwritten letter addressed to Pope Pius IX, a black woman from New York described the situation of black Catholics in New York City. The letter is noteworthy because it revealed the attitude and mentality of black laypersons in a city where Catholicism was found mainly among the large Irish immigrant society. As was the case of black Catholics in Philadelphia almost forty years before, black Catholics spoke in passionate terms about the lack of a Catholic education for their children. With deliberate frankness, this very articulate woman spoke about the attitude towards blacks by the archbishop of New York, John J. Hughes (1779–1864). The punctuation has been corrected and the text has been improved.

New York, October 29th 1853

Most Holy Father Visible Head of the Church of Jesus Christ.

I humbly write these lines to beseech your Holiness in the name of the same Saviour if you will provide for the salvation of the black race in the United States who is going astray from neglect on the part of those who have the care of souls. Now I would not dare to say anything disrespectful against the ministers of God but the reason of this neglect is, as it is well known to your Holiness, that most of the Bishops and priests in this country is either Irish or descended from Irish and not being accustomed to the black race in Ireland they can't think enough of them to take charge of our souls. Hence it is a great mistake to say that the church watched with equal care over every race and color, for how can it be said they teach all nations when they will not let the black race mix with the white. We know that this teaching does not mean high learning but means a teaching of Holy Doctrine. But in this country the teaching of the word of God and learning is so closely connected together that he who receives the one receives the other. The Catholics teach the pure word of God and gave learning at the same time. The Protestants gave learning and teach the word of God adulterated.

Now the Protestant rule in the city and county of New York is that all poor children in every district no matter what color they are must attend the State schools. A very good rule too, but the evil overshadows the good. Those are the evils: as soon as the teachers find any children in these schools to be Catholics they teach them directly to protest against the church of God. They tell them that the Blessed Eucharist is nothing but a wafer, that the priest drinks the wine himself and gives the bread to us, and that the Divine institution of confession is only to make money and that the Roman pontiff is Anti-Christ. This is what Catholic children are taught in Protestant Schools, but the church [can] remedy these evils for the white children by providing schools where they can learn the pure word of God and how to keep it. But the church do[es] leave the colored children a prey to the wolf. Now the Protestants well know that the Catholics do not like the black race with them neither in the churches nor schools. Hence they take the advantage of the opportunity....

Yes, Holy Father this is precisely the conditions of the colored Catholics in most of the United States... but particularly in New York. If your Holiness's Nuncio were to condescend while he is here to inquire about the colored people he would find many families with the parents Catholics and the children Protestants, overwhelmed with the belief that the name of Catholic amongst the black race will in a few years fall away....[1]

Yes Most Holy Father if I was to write this out of disrespect or to give scandal I would deserve punishment from God and from your Holiness, but I do not mean disrespect. I only write it to pray your Holiness to take charge of us, Most Holy Father. I pray you will pardon my liberty for writing this

---

1. The nuncio was Archbishop Gaetano Bedini (1806–64), who had been sent by Rome at this time to see whether it was feasible to establish a nunciature in the United States.

letter but every word is true. I hope if it is the will of God for the black race to be saved something will soon take place for the better....

> From Harriet...Thompson
> College Place
> New York City.

There were twenty-six signers of this letter.

Congregation of the Propaganda Archives, University of Notre Dame, microfilm. Scritture Riferite nei Congressi: America Centrale, vol. 16, fols. 770rv–775r. See Finbar Kenneally, *United States Documents in the Propaganda Archives* (Washington, D.C.: Academy of American Franciscan History, 1981), 2:113, no. 715, with permission.

14. Letter of William Henry Elder, Bishop of Natchez, to the Society for the Propagation of the Faith, in Which He Describes His Ministry to Slaves, 1858

William Henry Elder (1819–1904) was born in a slaveholding family in Maryland. He served as bishop of Natchez from 1857 to 1878, which included the Civil War. Despite his background, he showed a keen interest in the African American population. Later as archbishop of Cincinnati, he would be one of the main supporters of the black Catholic congress movement. In the following letter, written for foreign consumption in order to raise funds, he manifests a very paternalistic tone. The sentiments expressed were typical of many ecclesiastics of the time.

Gentlemen,

The business of my Diocese has made it necessary for me to spend much time in travelling. I have now been absent from home nearly two months continually, and in the spring likewise I was nearly two months away. Hence it has been impossible for me to write to you earlier as I had intended; and even now I cannot give you the full and interesting account of our missions which I had hoped to prepare, both from want of time on my own part, and because I have not got reports from the Pastors on the various points on which I would desire to inform you. Moreover, being obliged even now to write at various times and in various places, without the facilities which I should have at home for rendering my letter into French, you must pardon [me] for simply writing to you in English.

...it is necessary for you to understand that more than half our population consists of *negro slaves*, who number 309,878, besides free negroes to the number of 930.

These poor negroes form in some respects my chief anxiety. I believe they are generally well cared for, so far as health and the necessaries of life are concerned. But for learning and practising religion, they have at present very little opportunity indeed. Commonly the Masters are well disposed to allow them religious instruction, and sometimes they pay Ministers to come and preach on the plantation. They do not like to let the negroes go to a public church, because there is danger of their misbehaving when they are away from home, and out of sight of the Overseer; and because various inconveniences result from the servants of one plantation mingling with those of another. Each master has something particular in his regulations and his method of management, and if the servants have free intercourse together, they are apt to make each other jealous and dissatisfied.

Some masters indeed object to having a Minister come to preach to their slaves, and they rather encourage some one of the blacks themselves to become a preacher for the rest. You may imagine what kind of religious instruction the poor creatures get.

Catholic masters of course are taught that it is their duty to furnish their slaves with opportunities for being well instructed, and for practising their religion. And here is my anxiety, that I cannot enable those masters to do their duty because there are not Priests enough. The negroes must be attended in a great measure on the plantation, but for the reasons given above, and because in our case there are so few churches; and even where there is a church, the negroes of four or five plantations would fill it up, and leave no room for the white, nor for the other negroes of the neighborhood. The Priest then must go to the plantations, and these are scattered at great distances through the country. All the Priests that I have are residing in congregations from which they cannot be absent long. We need a band of traveling Missionaries who should attend to these plantations, and at the same time hunt out the Catholics scattered through the country. In both of these ways an immensity of good can be done. The poor negroes very often have at first a fear of a Catholic Priest, or imagine they can never understand him; but they are not ill disposed towards religion. Indeed they often have a craving for its ministrations. Having few comforts and no expectations in this world, their thoughts and desires are the more easily drawn to the good things of the world to come. I say often because often again they are so entirely animal in their inclinations, so engrossed with the senses, that they have no regard for any thing above the gratifications of the body. But even among such as these, the missionary often finds a good soil for the seed of religion, because their sensuality arises not so much from malice, as from the want of religious instruction — the want of knowing that there is anything better than this world within their reach. It is true, when from this ignorance they have formed habits of sin, they are not always ready to abandon them when better instructed; but patient and persevering instruction and exhortation, together with the use of the Sacraments, will commonly succeed at last in bringing them to a better life.

For the negro is naturally inclined to be dependent on others; therefore he is disposed to listen and believe what he is told by his superiors. When he resists the teachings of religion, it is not so much from stubbornness as from weakness of mind and will. This weakness of mind makes it hard for him to understand an argument; his weakness of will makes it hard to resist temptation, and still harder to break bad habits. It makes him also liable to great fickleness. This is one of the hard trials of a missionary among them. It is not uncommon for a negro to attend religious instruction for a considerable time with great fidelity and a lively interest, and yet drop off before receiving the Sacraments. Sometimes there is no apparent cause, but just fickleness of character, or perhaps secret temptation. But more generally it may be traced to some irregularity in the instruction, or some little neglect which begets an indifference on their part. They are very much creatures of feeling. If they are attended to regularly and if their instructor takes great interest in them, and gets them to realize the value of their souls, he can do a great deal with them for the glory of God. And he may have the unspeakable consolation of finding among them vocations to a high degree of sanctity. The humility of their condition and the docility of their character takes away many of the ordinary obstacles to the workings of grace; and where other circumstances are favourable, these lowly ones in the eyes of the world sometimes rise very high in the favour of God. I have known a case of a servant girl's being really revered as a saint by the family in which she had been reared, and where she was working with all simplicity and fidelity in the lowest offices.

Oh! what a harvest of souls among these 310,000 negroes; every one of them immortal, made to the image and likeness of God, redeemed by the Precious Blood of the Son of God! Oh! what a frightful havoc Satan is making among them! What numbers of children die without baptism! how many grown persons live and die in ignorance of God, and still worse, buried in miserable sins and habits of sins, which neither know nor care to free themselves from. Oh! for a band of Apostles like Fr. Claver,[1] to devote themselves to the service of the negro. Not such service indeed as he rendered to them with so much heroism; for our blacks are not often in that bodily wretchedness which called forth so much of his charity. They need services less repugnant to flesh and blood, and not less fruitful in the saving of souls and promoting the glory of God. They need instructions and the

---

1. St. Peter Claver (ca. 1580–1654), a Jesuit priest from Verdú in Spain who ministered to the African slaves arriving in Cartagena in present-day Colombia. He worked for over forty years in this ministry. [Ed.]

Sacraments. The Masters provide for their bodies and even in a great measure for their exterior conduct. Are there not Priests of God — at least in the generous Apostolic land of France — are there not still some there, who are ready to put the sickle into this abundant field? It will cost pains and patience, but the consolations will be very great, as they gather those rich sheaves of more than golden fruit into the granary of heaven. . . .

John Tracy Ellis, *Documents of American Catholic History* (Wilmington, Del: Michael Glazier, 1987), 1:325–29. The original document is in the Archives of the Diocese of Natchez, with permission.

15. The Defense of Slavery: The Pastoral Letter of Monsignor the Bishop of Natchitoches on the Occasion of the War of the South for Its Independence, 1861

The American bishops refused to take any concerted action regarding the slavery issue. Unlike other religious leaders, they refused to see any moral dimensions to the question of slavery. They insisted that it was a political question, which they would not address. Certain bishops did, however, defend slavery on the grounds that neither Christ nor the Apostles condemned it; that indeed the Church in past centuries had addressed the issue without condemning it in either synodal decrees or in Canon Law. Bishop John England (1786–1842) of Charleston, South Carolina, wrote eighteen letters to prove that the Catholic Church had never condemned slavery. The letters were published in 1840 and 1841 in the diocesan newspaper, U.S. Catholic Miscellany, *the first diocesan newspaper in the country. Auguste Martin (1803–75), the first bishop of Natchitoches in Louisiana, wrote a pastoral letter in August 1861 to the faithful in his diocese in which among other things he sought to show how the enslavement of Africans fit into God's plans. His letter was delated to Rome and was judged as being contrary to the teaching of Pope Gregory XVI, who had condemned the slave trade and slavery. It was decided that the bishop should have the opportunity of correcting his letter. In the end, the Civil War with the end of slavery rendered the condemnation moot. Following is an excerpt of his letter which was written originally in French.*

With the admirable provisions taken in His Providence, the Lord, the Father of us all, God who loves the souls for whom He gave his beloved and only Son and who makes use of simply human interests for eternal interests, for centuries has been snatching from the barbarity of their ferocious customs thousands of children of the race of Canaan, upon whom the curse of an outraged Father continues to weigh heavily, almost everywhere.

He commits them to the care of the privileged ones of the great human family for His own purposes and these people must be their shepherds and their fathers rather than their masters. The will of God regarding these poor men is manifest and it becomes clearly evident from the teaching of the Gospel itself. Those who have received from God the Faith of Jesus Christ, His grace and His eternal hopes, must share with their poor brothers a fair part of Heaven's gifts, which we all have freely received; so also he who has plenty of earthly goods is to relieve the needs of the poor with his wealth.

The manifest will of God is that, in exchange for a freedom which they are unable to defend and which will kill them, and in return for a lifetime of work, we must give these unfortunate people not only the bread and the clothes necessary to their material life but also, and especially their just share of truth and of the goods of grace, which may console them for their present troubles with the hope of eternal rest in the bosom of their Father, who calls them as well as us....

Maria Caravaglios, "A Roman Critique of the Pro-Slavery Views of Bishop Martin of Natchitoches, Louisiana," *Records of the American Catholic Historical Society of Philadelphia* 83 (1972): 71, with permission.

16. In Defense of Slavery: A Tract for the Times, Slavery and Abolitionism Being the Substance of a Sermon Preached in the Church of St. Augustine, Florida, on the 4th Day of January, 1861, Day of Public Humiliation, Fasting, and Prayer, by the Right Reverend A. Verot, D.D., Vicar Apostolic of Florida, 1861

Augustin Verot was Vicar Apostolic of Florida on January 4, 1861, when he preached a sermon in St. Augustine on the occasion of the day of fasting and prayer proclaimed by President Buchanan as the conflict between North and South seemed imminent. In this sermon, which he later published as a pamphlet, Verot defended slavery because it was sanctioned by the Church and society down through the centuries. In the second half of his sermon, he calls on the South to reform the slavery system and to do away with the injustices found in the institution. He expressed the notion that if slavery as an institution were not made more just and humane, then God would abandon the South.

...I must now, brethren, pass to the second part of my discourse, and having shown the lawfulness of Slavery in general, I must show the conditions upon which this state of things receives the sanction of justice, of God himself, and of the church — the visible guide given us by Our Lord Jesus Christ. It is in this part that I may have to mention wrongs which the South ought to acknowledge and confess; and if these wrongs be persevered in, this may be the reason why the Almighty, in his justice and wise severity, may sweep Slavery out of the land, not because Slavery is bad in itself, but because men will abuse it through wanton malice. The necessity of some conditions for the legitimacy of Slavery must appear evident to everybody. A man by being a slave, does not cease to be a man, retaining all the properties, qualities, attributes, duties, rights, and responsibilities attached to human nature, or to a being endowed with reason and understanding, and made to the image and likeness of God. A master has not over a slave the same rights which he has over an animal, and whoever would view his slaves merely as beasts, would have virtually abjured human nature, and would deserve to be expelled from human society. I will then state the various conditions which must accompany a legitimate possession of slaves.

In the first place it is domestic Slavery which we advocate to be lawful, and to have the sanction of God himself, but it is not the "slave-trade," or the African trade. The slave-trade is absolutely immoral and unjust, and is against all law natural, divine, ecclesiastical and civil. The slave-trade consists in kidnapping negroes by fraud and violence on the coasts of Africa, and bringing them to America for sale. This trade is evidently condemned by justice and humanity. What right has any man to steal another man and enslave him? This, next to murder, seems to be the grossest violence of justice that can be conceived....

Hence the slave-trade has been most severely prohibited by nearly all European Governments; it is, as all know, expressly forbidden by the United States....As to the ecclesiastical law, his Holiness, Gregory XVI, in the year 1839, issued apostolic letters forbidding most expressly this shameful commerce, forbidding any one to teach that it is lawful....

Here is another condition I must mention in the name of morality, in the name of public decency, in the name of religion, in the name of Christianity: it is that the whites do not take advantage of the weakness, ignorance, dependence, and lowly position of colored females, whether slaves or not — availing themselves of the impunity which, hitherto, laws in the South have extended to this sort of iniquity. It is indeed right that the two races should be kept distinct, and public sentiment repudiates amalgamation, and hence such connubial alliances are not to be encouraged and formed. But, things being on that footing, every outrage against morals should be repressed. It is the duty of the clergy to protest against every violation of the moral law.

This leads me to another condition on a subject kindred to the preceding. It is that matrimonial relations be observed among slaves, and that the laws of marriage be enforced among them. All know that there have been and there are frightful abuses about this point, and I leave it to the conscience, reason, and good sense of any upright and virtuous man, whether God can bless a country and a state of things in which there is a woeful disregard of the holy laws of marriage. It is our duty to proclaim to masters that they have indeed rights on the labor of their slaves; they can justly require of them obedience, respect, and service. But they are not the masters of their slaves in such a way that they can forbid them marriage, or prescribe it at pleasure....

United States Documents in the Propaganda Fide Archives, first series, vol. 3, p. 77, no. 489, fol. 1266–67, Archives of the University of Notre Dame, microfilm, with permission.

17. The Catholic Opposition to Slavery: *In Supremo Apostolatus Fastigio,* 1839

In 1839, Pope Gregory XVI (1831–46) wrote an apostolic brief in which he joined the major European powers in opposing the slave trade. This was one of the strongest pontifical documents opposing slavery. Its influence was minimal in the United States.

Pope Gregory XVI: For perpetual memory.

Since, through no merits of our own. We have been placed at the highest point of the Apostolate as Vicar of Jesus Christ the Son of God, Who because of His great charity willed to become man and die for the redemption of the world. We consider it to belong to our pastoral solicitude to avert the faithful from the inhuman trade in Negroes and all other groups of humans. Surely, since the light of the Gospel was first spread abroad, those unfortunate people who in such great numbers, and due especially to war had fallen into very cruel slavery, have experienced some relief especially when they were among Christians. Inspired by the Divine Spirit, the Apostles indeed urged slaves themselves to obey their masters according to the flesh as though obeying Christ, and to do the Will of God from their heart. However, the Apostles ordered the masters to act well towards their slaves, to give them what was just and equitable, and to refrain from threats, knowing that the Lord in heaven, with Whom there is no partiality in respect to persons, is indeed Lord of the slaves and of themselves. Indeed, since a sincere charity towards all was commended by the law of the Gospel, and since Our Lord Jesus Christ had declared that He considered as done or refused to Himself everything kind and merciful done or refused to the small and needy, it readily follows not only that Christians should regard as brothers their slaves, especially their Christian slaves, but that they should be more inclined to set free those who deserve it. Indeed this was the custom especially upon the occasion of the Easter Feast as Gregory of Nyssa tells us. Nor were there lacking Christians, who, moved by an ardent charity delivered themselves into captivity in order to redeem others. That Apostolic man, our predecessor of holy memory, Clement I, testified that he himself knew many instances of this. Therefore, in the course of time, when the darkness of pagan superstition was more fully dissipated and the customs of the uneducated people had been mitigated due to Faith operating by charity, it at last came about that, for several centuries now, there have been no slaves in the greater number of Christian peoples. But, We still say it with sorrow, there were to be found subsequently among the faithful some who, shamefully blinded by the desire of sordid gain, in lonely and distant countries, did not hesitate to reduce to slavery Indians, Blacks and other unfortunate peoples, or else, by instituting or expanding the trade in those who had been made slaves by others, aided the crime of others. Certainly many Roman Pontiffs of glorious memory, Our Predecessors, did not fail, according to the duties of their office, to blame severely this way of acting as dangerous for the spiritual welfare of those who did such things and a shame to the Christian name. They foresaw that it would follow from such activity that the peoples who did not have the Faith would be more and more confirmed in their hatred of the true Religion. It is to these practices that the Apostolic Letters of Paul III...and...another more detailed Letter...by Urban VIII...are severely and particularly condemned those who would dare to reduce to slavery the Indians of the Western and Southern Indies, sell them, buy them, exchange them or give them away, separate them from their wives and children, despoil them of their property, conduct or transport them into other regions, or deprive them of liberty in any way whatsoever, retain them in servitude, or lend counsel, aid, favor and help to those acting this way, no matter what the pretense or excuse. Like wise reprobated is anyone who proclaims and teaches that this way of acting is permissible and who co-operates in any manner whatever in the practices mentioned.

Benedict XIV afterwards confirmed and renewed the sanction of the said Popes...Pius II...[took] grave notice of those Christians who were reducing neophytes to slavery. In our time Pius VII, moved by the same religious and charitable spirit as his Predecessors, dutifully used his good offices with those in power to end completely the slave trade at least among Christians. Indeed these sanctions and this concern of Our Predecessors availed in no small measure, with the help of God, to protect the Indians and the other peoples mentioned from the cruelties of the invaders and from the greed of Christian traders: it was not such, however, that the Holy See could rejoice over the complete success of its efforts in this matter. The slave trade although it has been somewhat diminished, is still carried on by numerous Christians. Therefore, desiring to remove such a great shame from all Christian peoples, having fully reflected on the whole question, having taken the advice of many of Our Venerable Brothers the Cardinals of the holy Roman Church, and walking in the footsteps of Our Predecessors, We, by apostolic authority, warn and strongly exhort in the Lord faithful Christians of every condition that no one in the future dare to bother unjustly, despoil of their possession, or reduce to slavery Indians, Blacks or other such peoples. Nor are they to lend aid and favor to those who give themselves up to these practices, or exercise that inhuman traffic by which the Blacks, as if they were not humans but rather mere animals, having been brought into slavery in no matter what way, are, without any distinction and contrary to the rights of justice and humanity, bought, sold and sometimes given over to the hardest labor, to which is added the fact that in the hope of gain, proposed by the first owners of the Blacks for this same trade, dissensions and almost perpetual conflicts have arisen in those regions.

We then, by Apostolic Authority, condemn all such practices as absolutely unworthy of the Christian name. By the same Authority We prohibit and strictly forbid any Ecclesiastic or lay person from presuming to defend as permissible this trade in Blacks under no matter what pretext or excuse, or from publishing or teaching in any manner whatsoever, in public or privately, opinions contrary to what We have set forth in these Apostolic Letters.

Moreover so that these letters may be known more easily by all, lest anyone pretend ignorance of them, We decree and order that they be published on the walls of the Basilica....Given at Rome at St. Mary Major, under the seal of the Fisherman on December 3, 1839, the ninth year of our pontificate.

> Text from Joel S. Panzer, *The Popes and Slavery* (New York: Alba House, 1996), appendix B, "Documents of the Papal Magisterium against Slavery," 97–102, with permission.

18. Daniel O'Connell's Address against Slavery, 1833

Daniel O'Connell (1775–1847), the great Irish statesman who was the first Irish Catholic to sit in the British Parliament since the Reformation, was passionately opposed to slavery and proudly asserted that he was an Abolitionist. He could not accept that most Irish Americans supported slavery and detested blacks. In many of his speeches before the antislavery conventions and elsewhere he had occasion to attack the slaveholders in the United States. The following is an extract from one of his speeches.

...I would adopt the language of the poet, but reverse the imagery, and say, "In the Deepest hell, there is a depth still more profound," and that is to be found in the conduct of the American slave owners.[1] They are the basest of the base — the most execrable of the execrable. I thank God, that upon the wings of the press, the voice of so humble an individual as myself will pass against the western breeze — that it will reach the rivers, the lakes, the mountains, and the glens of America — and that the friends of liberty there will sympathize with me, and rejoice that I here tear down the image of Liberty from the recreant hand of America, and condemn her as the vilest of hypocrites — the greatest of liars.

When this country most unjustly and tyrannically oppressed its colonies, and insisted that a Parliament of borough-mongers in Westminster should have the power of putting their long fingers across the Atlantic into the pockets of the Americans, taking out as much as they pleased, and, if they found anything, leaving what residuum they chose — America turned round and appealed to justice, and she was right: appealed to humanity, and she was right; appealed to her own brave sword, and she was right, and I glory in it. At that awful period, when America was exciting all the nations of the world; when she was declaring her independence, and her inhabitants pledged their lives, their fortunes, and their sacred honor, and invoked the God of charity (whom they foolishly called the God of battles, which he is not, any more than he is the God of murder) — at that awful period, when they laid the foundation of their liberty, they began with these words: "We behold [*sic*] these truths to be self-evident; that all men are created equal; that they are endowed by their Creator with certain inalienable rights; that among these are life, liberty, and the pursuit of happiness." The American has acknowledged what he cannot deny, viz., that God the Creator has endowed man with those inalienable rights. But it is, not the white man, it is not the copper-colored man, nor is it the black man alone, who is thus endowed; it is all men who are possessed of these inalienable rights. The man, however, who cannot vote in any State assembly without admitting this as the foundation of his liberty, has the atrocious injustice, the murderous injustice, to trample upon these inalienable rights as it were, to attempt to rob the Creator of his gifts, and to appropriate to himself his brother man, as if he could be his slave. Shame be upon America! eternal shame be upon her escutcheon! ...

The voice of Europe will proclaim the slave's deliverance, and will say to him, "Shed no blood, but take care that your blood be not shed." I tell the American slave-owner, that he shall not have silence; for, humble as I am, and feeble as my voice may be, yet deafening the sound of the westerly

---

1. Inasmuch as these extracts were copies of the speeches delivered live, the reporters placed in the text "(cheers)" to indicate audience reaction; these indications have been omitted. [Ed.]

wave, and riding against the blast as thunder goes, it shall reach America, telling the black man that the time for his emancipation has come, and the oppressor that the period of his injustice is soon to terminate!

Speech delivered at the Great Anti-Colonization Meeting in London, 1833, microfilm collection, 44456 E. Library of Congress, Washington, D.C.

19. Public Letter of Augustin Cochin, Catholic Abolitionist, against American Slavery, to Albert, Duc de Broglie, 1863

Augustin Cochin (1823–72) was a devout Catholic layman, who belonged to the liberal wing of Catholicism in nineteenth-century France, along with Count Charles de Montalembert, Count Albert de Broglie, Henri Lacordaire, O.P., and others. Cochin was an opponent of slavery and wrote against it.[1] The following is from the introduction to one of his antislavery works.

In the United States, strange moralists affirm that slavery elevates the intelligence of the possessing race, and, freeing it from all cares, devotes it to the pursuit of noble mental labors, communicates to it the governing qualities, and expands the heart, constantly moved by the spectacle of weak and imperfect beings, whilst, discharging society from the burden of these weak beings, it places them under the patronage of the best citizens, who rear, guide, and assist them; a beneficent and productive organization, superior to every combination of relations between rich and poor presented in the history of the world! Experience, pitiless experience, replies, that the master becomes hard, indolent, and sensual; that the habit of command takes away all cordiality even towards free working men; that it leads to confounding in the same contempt the labor and the laborer; that the plus value of lands cultivated by free labor exceeds the capital represented by slaves; that the human intellect is developed only through activity, — that passive, it slumbers, — constrained, it becomes soured or degraded. In a word, in this detestable system, the owner becomes a beast of prey, the owned a beast of burden, the master is without calculation, the workman without progress; time, far from ameliorating this position, aggravates it; with time, instruction, the pretext of slavery, is interdicted by law; the separation of classes widens and becomes envenomed; prejudice, created by slavery, survives it to the degree that the North refuses equality to the black, while the South refuses him liberty; the pretended political superiority of the South is only the unanimous and persevering resolution to sacrifice to the maintenance of the *peculiar institution*, everything, even honor, even peace, even country. The sacrifice is made, the war declared, — not a war between slave and

---

1. The most important work is *L'Abolition de l'Esclavage,* for which Pope Pius IX decorated him.

master, but between whites, between brethren, between fellow-citizens, — war against justice and nature, — civil war!

Servitude is a poisoned river, flowing into evil from which it takes its rise. Whilst its fatal consequences are rending America, another continent, Africa, suffers from its criminal origin.

Augustin Cochin, *The Results of Emancipation,* trans. Mary L. Booth (Boston: Walker, Wise, 1863), 17–18.

20. Letter of Monsignor the Bishop of Orléans to the Clergy of His Diocese on Slavery, 1862

Félix-Antoine-Philibert Dupanloup (1802–78), bishop of Orléans, was one of the most influential Catholic bishops of his time. He played a leading role in the political conflicts between the Church and State in nineteenth-century France. His pastoral letter carried a great deal of weight in the public opinion of the time.

Gentlemen and Co-Workers,

During Lent you do not dwell in your rectory, all day you dwell in your church: you hold yourself standing, so to speak, before men and on your knees before God, in order to preach and in order to pray, calling upon men the gaze of God and his pardon; beseeching the people to meditate with you the death of Jesus Christ, and to unite to the sufferings of the cross the sufferings of their lives. Into the midst of your pious duties, I do not come to bring a distraction; I come to solicit a prayer.

Prayer is our political policy; it is our great part in the events of this world. To speak of God to men and women and to speak of them to God is our mission. And certainly, it is no small thing, even in the order of earthly interests, which is fought about with so much passion among men. For, in the end, it is God who holds in his hands the hearts of the people and of kings, and inclines them where he wishes.

Today, Passion Sunday, at this hour in which the standard of the cross is raised aloft in our temples, in the sight of this sacred sign of deliverance and salvation, I say to myself: My God has died on the cross for all; and however there are those who are still on the cross! He has died to deliver all from servitude; and there are those — the noise which is made at the moment about this great question recalls it to me with sorrow — there are a thousand persons who are still in slavery!

… is it not St. Paul, one of the most fervent of disciples, who cried to the pagan world this sublime cry: "There are no more masters and slaves, for we are all brothers in Jesus Christ" (Galatians, 3:28).

Very well, still today on Christian lands, after eighteen centuries of Christianity after the words of Jesus Christ, after the cry of St. Paul, there are still slaves!

Gentlemen, it is for this miserable and cruelly oppressed portion of humanity that I come to ask you to pray: yes, let us pray; let us pray for the poor slaves!

And if I feel myself so pressured at this hour to recommend to you this sad and holy cause, and to solicit your prayers, it is because of these holy days in which we are now and also by this recent news arrived in this country where this sad matter is a question and towards which are turned the gaze of Europe.

The truth is that the ancient and the new continents are moved: politicians speak for and against; the commerce is troubled; blood flows in civil war; we, gentlemen, pray. In the great social crises, in which we can no longer remain indifferent spectators, it is prayer especially which is our great duty.

Do not expect, Gentlemen, that I shall take part in the lamentable quarrel which divides the United States of America. They tell me that the North merits not much more sympathy than the South; that the questions of commercial tariffs or of political predominance have more influence than the question of slavery on the split from which the civil war has issued. They have assured me that the party of abolition is rendered more odious by its excesses while the masters are of good faith and often of good heart.

They show me more Catholics of the South than in the North; and of the citizens engaged in the two armies with an equal patriotism, who sincerely believe from the two sides that they serve justice.

They say that if the Union is reformed the liberation of the slaves is not certain; and that if the separation is accomplished, this liberation is not impossible. They wish to persuade me that the interests of our industry lie with the South; those of our commerce with the North; that we ought to desire the maintenance and the union of one nation that we have contributed to set free and which serves as a counterweight to other nations; or very well on the contrary that we ought to fear the aggrandizement of a people whose example and the invading spirit menaces the world.

Of this I know nothing, but what I do know is that there are still four million slaves in the United States, two million in the rest of America, in all six million slaves on Christian lands, eighteen centuries after the cross. What I do know is that the horrors of war have been unleashed by this redoubtable question, and that the peace of the world is menaced and already troubled by it.

And what I am more happy in knowing is that by a recent and important act, a message of March 8th, brought to the Congress by the president of the United States, and voted and adopted by a great majority, regular, equitable, peaceful measures have been proposed to put an end to slavery....

I know the objections of those who plead on behalf of slavery: I do not at all wish to discuss them at length. No, let no one tell me that the slaves are happy and that besides accomplished facts become legitimate after a long period of time.

The slaves are happy. Perhaps yes, in the homes of better off slave owners, they sleep, have several hours of leisure; perhaps even be corrupted with pleasure. But have they the family hearth? Have they a family? Have they fatherhood? Have they freedom? Poor disinherited of the human family, have they lost not only the privilege of the eldest son but all of their rights? And because they have still left to them the dish of lentils, they proclaim that they are happy!...

Let no one ask me to discuss the theoretical question of slavery. Let no one recall that all the ancient societies have passed this way. Let no one at all seek to demonstrate to me, by force of unrealizable hypotheses, that slavery is not illicit in itself, considered from a certain point of view under certain conditions.

I lay aside abstract theory, and I look at the facts. I look at how many times these conditions have been met in history and how, humanity being given what it is, they can be met. I look not at the exceptional case but the state, the foundation even of life and human dignity, condemned by slavery to an irremediable abasement.

I do not care about abstractions and hypotheses. I certainly would have much to say on the origin of this obstinate plague, so widespread and so ancient. How is it that man could reduce a man to slavery? I defy that they explain this to me without original sin. How has the slave become the equal of the owner? I defy that they explain this without the Redemption. Slavery is so detestable that one cannot comprehend the beginning, and it is so easy that one does not understand the end.

If I were to venture the theory, I would show that the unity of the human family, which is for us not an opinion but a dogma — let it be understood well, a dogma, and one of the foundations even of our Faith has become also a dogma of science. I would show that the unity of the human family, the principle of dignity, of equality, of liberty, of humanity among persons, condemns and rejects slavery....

There are then on the same earth as I, children of God and sons and daughters of men as well as I, saved by the same blood as I, destined to the same heaven as I, five or six million of those like me in the United States, in

Brazil, in Cuba, in Surinam, who are slaves: elderly people, men, women, young girls, and children.

Just Heaven! Is it not finally time after eighteen hundred years of Christianity that we all begin to practice the eternal law: Do not do to another what you do not wish that it be done to yourself! And what you would wish that your brothers should do for you, do it for them (Matthew 7:12)....

Félix, Bishop of Orléans

Orléans, Passion Sunday, April 6, 1862.

Published text obtained from the Diocese of Orléans, France.

Part 3

CONGREGATIONS
OF BLACK SISTERS

Before the end of slavery, several attempts were made to establish a religious community of black sisters. Only two succeeded: one in Baltimore in the 1820s and the second in New Orleans in the 1840s. A third community of black sisters was established in Savannah in the first quarter of the twentieth century. These religious communities of black women demonstrate the spiritual vitality of the black Catholic community in the slavery states of Maryland and Louisiana. Some of the women, freed slaves, who entered the convent in Baltimore came to the cloister with their manumission papers in their hand. Religious vocations emerge from the religious understanding of a people. These women were the faith-filled daughters of a faithful people in a society and even in a church where they were often not valued. On the other hand, these early communities of black women are the first examples of religious orders that were totally American in origin and organization with no ties to a European motherhouse. Finally, they are the living example of how the evangelization of African Americans was from its beginning the work of both white Catholics and black Catholics.

21. From the "Journal of the Sisters of Providence," 1829

The Oblate Sisters of Providence was founded in Baltimore in 1829 by four black Haitian women, Elizabeth Lange, Marie Balas, Rosine Boegue, and Almeide Maxis Duchemin, with the collaboration of Jacques Joubert de la Muraille. The following is a section from the "Journal of the Sisters of Providence," a record of the first years of the congregation, written in French by Jacques Joubert, their chaplain.

5 June 1829
In spite of the approbation which was given by Archbishop Whitfield, these good girls remained uneasy and very discouraged. They admitted to me that after all they had heard said, only through obedience would they be determined to take the religious habit. I had myself heard such talk. I knew

Mother Mary Elizabeth Lange, O.S.P. (c. 1784–1882). Co-founder with Fr. Jacques Joubert, S.S., of the Oblate Sisters of Providence. Reprinted with permission of the Archives of the Josephite Fathers, Baltimore.

already that many persons who had approved the idea of a school for pupils disapproved very strongly that of forming a religious house, and could not think of the idea of seeing these poor girls (colored girls) wearing the religious habit, and constituting a religious community. I made them understand that it was their duty to inform me of all these reports, and that difficulties were usual in the beginning of every kind of establishment. That they should rest on the purity of their intentions, and since their actions were misinterpreted by certain persons, they should put all their confidence in God; that until now their work seemed good, so they must not stop because of the judgment of men who often judge things through their passions and prejudices.

17 June 1829

I was not without a certain fear myself, and I resolved to make known all of this to the Archbishop. To this effect, I made a visit to him on June 17th. I told him all my fears, but I found him perfectly at ease about this affair. He knew very much himself, more than I did, and he advised me not to be in the least discouraged. He said: "Monsieur Joubert, it is not lightly but with reflection that I approved your project. I knew and saw the finger of God; let us not oppose his holy will. I have heard all that is being said. Besides, have I not the power to make foundations in my diocese, in my Episcopal City, any religious establishment whatsoever? Yours is unique in its kind, it should not have resentment from anyone. I engage you, I command you even, to continue the work you have undertaken. I promise to protect this new foundation. The day will come when justice will be rendered you; it is the will of God that you be agitated; it is for His greater glory; it will be manifested one day. Go peacefully, humbly and do not pay any attention to anything that may be said." I followed constantly the advice of the Archbishop in all that I did. I recommended the good Sisters to act with all humility and confidence in God. I told them of the conversation I had had with Archbishop Whitfield and the encouragement he gave us; they should return thanks to Our Lord, and from that moment they began preparing for the great oblation they desired to make on the following July 2nd, the Feast of the Visitation of the Blessed Virgin who was chosen the first patroness of their house.

In 1835, the superior of the Sulpician seminary in Baltimore requested two sisters to serve as housekeepers in the seminary. The request presented a dilemma. The Oblate Sisters were all black. In a state where slavery was well established it was considered normal that black women be domestics. On the other hand, the Oblate Sisters wished to be religious sisters. They wished to be recognized as sisters whose major work was teaching. The other side of the dilemma was the fact that the Sulpicians had served as their spiritual directors and chaplains. The answer to the superior of the seminary was a carefully worded acceptance of the request with a statement of their identity as religious women.

20 September 1835

Copy of letter written to Rev. Msgr. Deluol, Superior of the Seminary, by the Oblate Sisters of Providence:

Reverend Superior:

After having reflected on the proposition that was made to us by you, Our Reverend Father, we think that we should be very happy to consent to what was asked of us. The gratitude that we owe you and so many of your priests, above all to Msgr. Tessier, and the charity which prompted you to protect us in diverse circumstances, will not allow us to refuse this occasion of obliging you. We find in this another advantage, that is the facility to care for Venerable Father Tessier in his old age, and Rev. Father Joubert, our Founder, our benefactor and our father, because it has been a great privation to us not to be able to render the services required by the age of one and the frequent illness of the other; but in your house we shall have this satisfaction. While Rev. Superior, we can not give our consent but under certain conditions, our sole wish is to do the Will of God. We have all prayed for enlightenment; we recommended this important affair to our good Mother and to our Holy Patrons. We made a general Communion for this intention this morning. We shall consequently humbly submit it to you, our reflections and requests. We do not conceal the difficulty of our situation. As persons of color and religious at the same time, and we wish to conciliate these two qualities in such a manner as not to appear too arrogant on the one hand and on the other, not to miss the respect which is due to the state we have embraced and the holy habit which we have the honor to wear. Our intention in consenting to your request is not to neglect the religious profession which we have embraced. Doubtless this was not your intention nor that of your priests. We wish to be able to follow in your seminary or in our house, the rules by which we live and are known to be Sisters. Consequently, not to have any other relation with the other servants and outside people than our obligations require. For this reason we should wish that the Sisters have some particular place in the seminary to take their meals and have the liberty to retire to the apartment assigned to them, as soon as they have finished their different duties which should oblige them to remain in the kitchen. In no case could they take charge of the office of porter or serve the table. In a house of men, a man should have charge of these two employments. We also take the liberty to change the two Sisters in that there would be not the same ones always or for too long a time....It is forbidden by our rule to visit or to receive visitors. We wish that an express prohibition be made in this regard for the kitchen of the seminary. We wish that this agreement be made in writing and that a copy be left at our house. If you agree, Rev. Superior, to all these conditions, we shall make a choice among the Sisters, which shall without doubt, receive your approbation and which shall prove the esteem which we hold your confidence that you have so readily placed in us.

> Your very humble and respectful servants,
> Oblate Sisters of Providence,
> (Signed) Sister Mary, Superior

29 September 1835

Sister Frances and Sister Rose entered the seminary this evening. We thought that the letter of the Superior and the copy of that which the Sisters had written to him on September 20th should answer instead of writing it again. The seminary shall pay each year to the convent of the Sisters of Providence one hundred and twenty dollars.

> Text from the English translation of the original diary of the Oblate Sisters of Providence, 1827–42, Archives of the Oblate Sisters, Baltimore, with permission.

22. The Journal of Sister Bernard Deggs: A History of the Sisters of the Holy Family, 1894

The second community of black sisters was founded in the 1840s in New Orleans by Henriette Delille (1812–62), a free woman of color, who with two other free women of color, Juliette Gaudin (1808–87) and Josephine Charles (1812–85), began to care for the aged poor, many of whom were abandoned elderly slaves; to teach catechism to the slaves; and to teach daughters of the free people of color. Their work developed gradually in a city that had the largest slave market in the South. In time the Sisters of the Holy Family became as much a part of the atmosphere and tradition of New Orleans as Mardi Gras. In 1894 one of the Sisters of the Holy Family, Sister Mary Bernard Deggs, began a history of the congregation from its inception up until her time. Although French was her native language, she wrote the text in English, a language that she did not know well. This history was more a celebration of the wonderful things that God had wrought in bringing the three women together. She wanted to show that God had worked within these women and their successors. In doing so we are able to see the feelings and dispositions of black women at the end of the nineteenth century.

Mother Henriette Delille (1812–62). Foundress of the Sisters of the Holy Family. Reprinted with permission of the Archives of the Sisters of the Holy Family, New Orleans.

These good sisters first came together in community in an old house on St. Bernard Street. They did not remain in that house but a few months. It was intended for a home for poor, aged women, but a wounded man was one day brought to them by the parish trustees. As they could not refuse to take him, both Henriette Delille and Juliette Gaudin retired to a small place on Bayou Road, and waited some twelve to eighteen months for good Father Rousselon to build them a house on Bayou Road near St. Claude Street. They lived there and did much good work from 1842 until 1883. Many were the souls brought to God in that humble house and many a pain and sorrow did the women pass in their first ten years, but they never lost hope. Many were the times that the foundresses had nothing to eat but cold hominy that had been left from some rich family's table. It is not necessary to say a word about their clothing, for it was more like Joseph's coat that was of many pieces and colors darned, until darn was not the word. In spite of the charity of their many kind friends, they suffered much owing to the strictness of the times....

In the old house on Chartres Street, Rev. Mother Josephine had both a night class and also a Latin and music class for young ladies whose means would not allow them to attend the day class as they wished. No one would believe which of the two classes worked the hardest. But for ourselves, we were better pleased with the night class, for to see them later is far better than those of the day.

These things occurred when we first opened the old St. Mary's School on Chartres Street in 1870, in a house that had been used for a trader's yard in the time of slavery. After the late war, many in this city looked on the old house as a disgraceful place and it was abandoned. No one would think of buying it for the very reason that it had previously been a trader's yard and many sins had been committed at that place, not only sins, but the most horrible crimes. It must have been the will of God that our sisters should buy the place to expiate the crimes that had been committed there. I think that was the reason Almighty God would not let anyone take a liking to the place. That was one of the most successful houses that the Holy Family Sisters ever had since its foundation. All of our most useful and able members have entered in that house. It was there that we completed the beautiful habit which we now have.

It is true that we had to suffer very much and to bear many crosses before we were able to obtain what we desired. So many years of pain and toil passed before we could find anyone to help our dear old Father Gilbert Raymond who also received a great many insults for our sake. He was told that he had just as well give up, for he would never be able to make anything out of us and that we would never do anything in this city, for we would never find any vocations among our class of people, who loved their pleasure so much.

Text from Sister Mary Bernard Deggs, *No Cross, No Crown: Black Nuns in Nineteenth-Century New Orleans*, ed. Virginia Meacham Gould and Charles E. Nolan (Bloomington: Indiana University Press, 2001), 8–9, 46, with permission.

Part 4

THE POST–CIVIL WAR PERIOD

At the close of the Civil War, the Catholic Church in the United States met in plenary council in 1866 in Baltimore. While many Christian Churches had split over the question of slavery, the Catholic Church remained undivided. Martin J. Spalding, archbishop of Baltimore, saw the council as a means for encouraging the evangelization of the freed slaves. The Roman curia concurred with this goal. They gave their support to a proposal to establish an ordinary who would oversee this ministry on a nationwide basis. The bishops, unaware that Spalding had made the original proposal, were enraged by what they considered to be an imposition placed on them by the Curia. They rejected the notion of a national ordinary. The matter was discussed at a stormy session on October 22, 1866. The minutes of this extraordinary session were never translated from the Latin nor published in the *Acta et Decreta*. The following is the copy of the summary of the Twenty-Ninth Extraordinary Session. It was published in Latin without any mention of the bitter fight that followed (*Concilii Plenarii Baltimorensis II: Acta et Decreta* [Baltimore: John Murphy, 1868], lxxxviii–lxxxix).

23. The Second Plenary Council of Baltimore, the Minutes of the Extraordinary Session, October 22, 1866

Since it could happen that bishops, already overworked with so many cares, might be impeded from applying their minds to procuring missionaries for this work, it would seem that there should be selected an ecclesiastical man, residing in Baltimore, or in another place if it should appear more expeditious, who should have entirely as his responsibility the procuring of missionary priests in sufficient number for the Negroes. It would be incumbent on him, when the Ordinaries should request it, to send workers into that part of the vineyard where there would be the greater work for them. To him all could apply who wished to undertake this Apostolic work; and to him would fall the duty of stirring up the zeal of priests by opportune incentives. If indeed it should so please the Supreme Pontiff, he could even be endowed with the Episcopal character, so that thus there might be regard for the honor of the office and his ministry be rendered more effective.

XXIX Extraordinary Private Session, Held on Monday, the 22nd of October

...For a long time this was discussed among the Fathers. They indicated readily indeed, that they wished to follow the mind of the Sacred Congregation; they were not, however, of one opinion as to the better way of attaining both their own intentions and those of the Holy See; while certain of them favored those points which were contained...about placing an ecclesiastical man in charge of this work, the majority preferred that the matter be left entirely to the bishops....

Original Minutes of the XXIX Extraordinary Private Session of the Second Plenary Council of Baltimore

...The archbishop of New Orleans (John Mary Odin) expressed the opinion that, just as he had done in the past, so also would he do in the future; he has always done everything for these people as he has for others, and he would continue to do so, only the number of missionaries would be increased; nothing further ought to be innovated.

With this the bishop of Savannah (Augustin Verot) did not at all agree, asserting that he wished something to be specially established by the Fathers, particularly when looking at the almost hopeless situation under which the Negro is laboring....He vehemently urged that an ecclesiastical man be put in charge of promoting the salvation of the Negroes.

...The bishop of Richmond (John McGill) recounted that there were many Negroes around him in the city of Richmond, although few believers. He made known that almost thirty Catholics could be found among them, although they were 10,000 and more in number. He could not at all understand how the Sacred Congregation could so act with the bishops, and he asserted that, under the appearance of truth, they had been led into an erroneous opinion....While the Negroes were still in a servile state, the Daughters of Charity under the rule of St. Vincent had gathered them together, whomsoever could be, and taught these people the rudiments of the faith; but the sisters had been prohibited in law whenever the Negroes were under the control of non-Catholic masters. Before the war it was therefore an impossible task for us, even though we were inclined towards it. He was entirely unwilling that a prefect of this type for the Negro Missions should be accepted....

The Most Reverend Apostolic Delegate (Martin Spalding) read to the group that Instruction which the Sacred Congregation had given, and spoke gravely of the necessity of following out the intention of the Sacred Congregation in this regard.

The bishop of Richmond (John McGill) replied that the Sacred Congregation had not well understood the true condition in our Provinces; they had been quite poorly informed by someone. The Most Reverend archbishop of St. Louis (Peter Richard Kenrick) firmly asserted that he would accept no such prefect; if indeed such a one were sent, he would renounce episcopacy; he was very little in favor of a divided administration for himself.

... The bishop of Richmond (John McGill) inquired whether or not something would be instituted by the Fathers in favor of our white People? ...

The bishop of Savannah (Augustin Verot) answered that the whole matter particularly being treated here was the Negroes, and that at the present time there should be no discussion on other things; the Church indeed wished all to become saved; but now, according to the mind of the Sacred Congregation, something special ought to be established for the Negroes.

... then the archbishop of St. Louis (Peter Kenrick) replied that bishops, who have fittingly done everything for their own people, are not to be publicly greeted with censure; but that if anything new should be established, it would seem as though the bishops had been deficient in their duty. Bishops have been placed by the holy Spirit to rule the Church of God, not to know the Instructions of Propaganda.

> 39A-D-5, Archives of the Archdiocese of Baltimore; the translation is from the Josephite Archives, Baltimore, with permission.

24. The Bishops' Pastoral Letter at the Close of the Second Plenary Council of Baltimore, 1866

The bishops of the United States published a pastoral letter at the close of the Second Plenary Council of Baltimore, October 21, 1866. In this letter mention is made of the emancipation of slaves. One cannot help but feel that the tone is cold and unfeeling.

We must all feel, beloved Brethren, that in some manner a new and most extensive field of charity and devotedness has been opened to us, by the emancipation of the immense slave population of the South. We could have wished, that in accordance with the action of the Catholic Church in past ages, in regard to the serfs of Europe, a more gradual system of emancipation could have been adopted, so that they might have been in some measure prepared to make a better use of their freedom, than they are likely to do now. Still the evils which must necessarily attend upon the sudden liberation of so large a multitude, with their peculiar dispositions and habits, only make the appeal to our Christian charity and zeal, presented by their forlorn condition, the more forcible and imperative.

We urge upon the Clergy and people of our charge the most generous co-operation with the plans which may be adopted by the Bishops of the Dioceses in which they are, to extend to them that Christian education and moral restraint which they so much stand in need of. Our only regret in regard to this matter is, that our means and opportunity of spreading over them the protecting and salutary influences of our holy Religion, are so restricted.

> "The Pastoral Letter of 1866," in *The National Pastorals of the American Hierarchy, 1792–1919,* ed. Peter Guilday (Washington, D.C.: National Catholic Welfare Council, 1925), 220–21.

25. America's First Black Catholic Priests: Bishop John B. Fitzpatrick, Bishop of Boston, to Archbishop John Hughes, Archbishop of New York, 1859

The first black Catholic priests in the history of the United States were the three sons of an Irish-American slaveholder, Michael Morris Healy, and his slave, Mary Eliza, who bore him ten children, nine of whom survived. Michael Morris Healy's children were all slaves according to the law. To save them from this condition, Michael Healy eventually arranged that his children would leave the South. With the help of John Fitzpatrick, who eventually became the bishop of Boston in 1846, three of Michael Healy's sons became students at Holy Cross College in Worcester, Massachusetts, and eventually were ordained priests. James Augustine Healy, the eldest son, was ordained for the diocese of Boston in 1854 and was made bishop of Portland, Maine, in 1875. The second son, Patrick Francis Healy, S.J., became the first president of Georgetown University in Washington, D.C., in 1874. At that time Georgetown University did not admit blacks as students. Alexander Sherwood Healy was also ordained for the diocese of Boston in 1858. Gifted and intelligent, he had a promising future, which unfortunately was cut short by his untimely death in 1875. The ability of Alexander Healy becomes evident when one realizes that at one time Bishop Williams went so far as to discuss the possibility that Alexander Healy could become the first rector of the North American College in Rome. A decade later Bishop Williams chose young Alexander Healy to be his personal theologian at the First Vatican Council, the first and only African American to serve in this capacity.

Boston, July 10, 1859

I have thought and thought upon the subject of your communication, the choice of a rector for the American College at Rome, and in the end I am as much puzzled to reach a practical conclusion as I was in the beginning. In reflecting upon the matter has not paused even for an instant upon any of the clergymen with whom I am well acquainted for I know not one in whom some deficiency is not evident at first glance. Amongst those with whom I am less intimate Rev. Mr. Hayden of Bedford Springs, Penn, arrests favorably my attention.... And yet there is a third man who in my opinion is admirably qualified for the office. But he is very young, just ordained, and wholly unknown to any of our prelates, except myself. That man is Alexander S. Healy, the brother of my present secretary. He has had the advantage of a most complete education from the Alphabet to Theology. He went through the entire course at St. Sulpice, Paris, where he was *facile princeps* [unquestionably first] in studies whilst he was at the same time a model of piety, regularity and good conduct. From Paris he went to Rome where he studied one or two years more and was ordained there at Easter. Still it would be useless to recommend him even were he known to the other Bishops as well as to myself. His youth would be a fatal objection. There is also another objection which though in reason less substantial, would in fact be quite as stubborn. He has african blood and it shews [*sic*] distinctly in his exterior. This, in a large number of american youths might lessen the respect they ought to feel for the first superior in a house....

I can think of nothing more to say upon the subject and I remain

With the most respectful attachment
Yr obedient Bro. in Xc.
+John Bernard Bp of Boston

Archives of the Archdiocese of New York, A-9, with permission.

26. Bishop Healy Excuses Himself from Attendance at the Third Black Catholic Congress in Philadelphia, 1891

Although the Healy brothers were all born slaves and as shown by the aforesaid document were seen as African Americans, the brothers did not identify themselves with the African American population. James Augustine Healy seems to have been quite ambivalent about the question of racial identity. In response to an invitation to participate in the third Black Catholic Congress in Philadelphia, he wrote the following letter to Father A. Stecker.

Reverend and dear Sir: It will be quite impossible for me to attend the convention to which you invite me on the 27th inst. I confess that I have some apprehension about conventions which are held on such strictly racial lines. But I trust that your convention and its results will make us all realize the words of St. Paul that we are of that Church where there is neither Gentile nor Jew; circumcision or uncircumcision; barbarian or Scythian, slave or free, but Christ is all and in all.

Yours very truly in Christ,
James A. Healy, Bishop of Portland

"Bishop Healy and the Colored Catholic Congress," *Interracial Review* 26–27 (1953–54): 79–80.

27. Father Augustus Tolton to John R. Slattery, S.S.J., on His Vocation, 1890

If James Augustine Healy and his brothers did not readily identify with the African American population, Augustus Tolton (1854–97) was seen by most black Catholics in the United States as their very own loved and revered priest. Tolton was ordained a priest in Rome in 1886. Pious, gentle, unassuming, he was made the pastor of black Catholics in Quincy, Illinois, in the diocese of Alton (now Springfield, Illinois). After the initial outpouring of celebration on his ordination to the priesthood by both whites and blacks in the city of Quincy, Tolton found himself the object of jealousy and anger on the part of the pastor of the neighboring parish. This violent attack seemed to have unnerved him and resulted in his request to leave the diocese of Alton and move to Chicago. In a letter from Chicago to Father John Slattery, S.S.J., the general of the Josephites, he described his situation and his sense of vocation. From the following letter it would seem that Father Slattery had requested him to give a lecture or preach at an African American church or congregation. Augustus Tolton did not use many punctuation marks or capital letters. These have been added.

2251 Indiana Avenue, Chicago, Ill.
Jan. 25th 1890

My dearest friend and Father Slattery

Rev. and dear friend.

Your kind letter has been just received and contents thoughtfully read. I must say that I wish at this moment that there were 27 Father Toltons or colored priests at any rate who could supply the demands, 27 letters at this moment asking me to come and lecture, come and give my kind assistance all of them speaking in the light. Yourself and Father McDermott's letters are of some weight I must confess, but now father Slattery what a grand

Father Augustus Tolton (1854–97) as a seminarian in Rome. Reprinted with permission of A. Rankin.

thing it would be if I were only a travelling missionary to go to all of the places that have called for me or what a grand thing if I were a Josephite belonging to your rank of missionaries. I could then get over America and accomplish some things; but here also I am hard at work. I have 27 _____ to work among here. One hundred families and [I] have just secured a site in which to build a church as soon as we have the means to begin one. So you see I am pushed now and a lot on the brain. I had to refuse going to St. Paul because I had too much to do going around getting up the names of my people and organizing a parish. For these poor people here who had been left in a bag with both ends open if I must say it. And the Archbishop has given them all up to me. He is an elegant Bishop. I love him. But I will promise you, Father Slattery, that if any jealousies arise here among the priests at my success, like in Quincy, I will put all of my books in the trunk and come right there to Baltimore and put myself in the hands of Father Leeson.[1] Then I know that I will be protected here in America. I was having too good a success in Quincy and the dutch priest could not stand it. Of course I left more for peace [*sic*] sake than anything else. I wrote to Rome first and got the Cardinal's consent[2] to come to Archbishop Feehan. I think I am safe now thanks be to God. So I being a new hand here in this diocese, I don't think it would be very nise [*sic*] in me going off now to the different places that have called for me. I have only been here 4 weeks. If you write to the Archbishop, I don't care if he says go I will go but he does not want me to slight these people here. So let all write to him and not to me and I will obey.

Your friend
A. Tolton
2251 Indiana Avenue, Chicago

9-S-16, Josephite Archives, Baltimore, with permission.

28. Father Tolton Writes St. Katherine Drexel, Foundress of the Sisters of the Blessed Sacrament, 1891

St. Katherine Drexel had used her inheritance to found a religious community of sisters who evangelized the Native Americans and the African Americans. Besides the ministry of her sisters, she personally distributed her wealth to special causes among the Indian Catholic missions and African American schools and parishes. The simplicity and the spirituality of Augustus Tolton is seen in the following two letters.

1. Alfred B. Leeson was provincial of the American Mill Hill Fathers, later to become the Josephites. [Ed.]

2. Giovanni Cardinal Simeoni (1816-92), prefect of the Congregation Propaganda Fide. [Ed.]

May 12th 1891
3554 Dearborn Street

My Dear Mother Catherine,

I am quite sure that you are bothered considerably now attending your own work and arranging matter for your new order which I am sure will be a blessing to our entire race. Father Stevan[1] asked me last week if I had written a letter. I told him I did then he says write again perhaps sister has forgotten you. I told him I did not think that you would forget us. Only I did not desire to be too hasty; we are glad that we can look forward in hopes. Here in Chicago we have so many promises but that will not help me. Still I must confess that I have done well to be here. Only 1 year and a half. I have together 260 souls to render an account of before God's majesty. There [are] all together 500 souls but they have become like unto the dead limbs on a tree. And without moisture because no one had taken care of them. Just Sunday night last I was called to the death bed of a colored woman who had been 9 years away from her duties because she was hurled out of a white church and even cursed at by the Irish members. Very bad indeed! She sent for me and thanked God that she had me to send for. These dear people feel proud that they have me to look after them. Even protestants when sick will send for me in preferance [sic] to their preachers and treat me with the greatest respects [sic]. Not one is prejudiced at all. That makes me feel like there is a great work for me. Sister, please answer if you have time enough to do it as I like very much to hear from you.

Rev. A. Tolton
3554 Dearborn Street
Chicago

Tolton to Mother Katherine, H 10 B Box 53, Archives of Sisters of the Blessed Sacrament, Bensalem, Pa., with permission.

June 5th 1891
3554 Dearborn Str., Chicago

Dear Mother Catherine,

I deem it necessary to write you this letter to ask to please forgive me for vexing you so; for one person, a priest of course, wrote me stating that all of us fathers on the colored missions were almost setting you crazy, that you had too many to tend to. I am sorry that I vexed you. Of course, I expected that letter from some one so I will apologize at once; of course, I for one cannot tell how to conduct myself when I see one person at least showing their love for the colored race. One thing I do know and that is it took the

---

1. This is probably Father J. A. Stephan, who was director of the Bureau of Indian Affairs in Washington, D.C. [Ed.]

Catholic Church 100 years here in America to show up such a person as yourself. That is the reason why you have so much bother now and many extending their hands to get a lift. In the whole history of the Church in America we can't find one person that has sworn to lay out their treasury for the sole benefit of the colored and Indians, as I stand alone as the first Negro priest of America. So you Mother Catherine stand alone as the first one to make such a sacrifice for the cause of a downtrodden race. Hence, the south is looking on with an angry eye. The north in many places is criticising [*sic*] every act, just as it is watching every move I make. I suppose that is the reason why we had no Negro priests before this day. They watch us, just the same as the Pharisees did our Lord. They watched him. I really feel that there will be a stirr [*sic*] all over the United States when I begin my church. I shall work and pull at it so long as God give me life, for I see that I have principalities to resist anywhere and everywhere I go. The world is indeed a great book, and I have read all of its pages. So this letter is to ask you to excuse me if I have bothered you too much. I know that you have a lot to do, for I am sure you have letters from all sides of America and even outside of it. Indian missionaries have always been writing to me for aid, but I could not render them any since I was in extreme need myself. But if I had anything to send them I would do so right off, but God has destined it this way, and I must be contented. Now, Sister, just when you get rested and get ready to send, all well and good. I will stop vexing your mind by my letters.

Respectfully,

A. Tolton
3554 Dearborn Str.
Chicago

Tolton to Mother Katherine, H 10 B Box 53, Archives of Sisters of the Blessed Sacrament, Bensalem, Pa., with permission.

29. Canon Benoît Notes in His Diary the Situation of Blacks in the United States, 1875

In 1871, four members of the newly established Mill Hill Fathers came from England and established themselves in Baltimore. The society was founded in 1866 as a missionary society by Herbert Vaughan, who later became archbishop of Westminster and cardinal. Martin J. Spalding, the archbishop of Baltimore, urged them to come to his diocese to work for the evangelization of black Americans. In 1893, under the leadership of John Slattery, the American members separated and became known as the Society of St. Joseph of the Sacred Heart.

In 1872, Herbert Vaughan visited many parts of the United States to ascertain the situation of blacks in this country. Three years later, Canon

Peter Benoît, the acting superior of the society, made an extensive journey throughout the South to survey the mission field. He recorded his experience in a journal, which was kept for the benefit of the then Bishop Vaughan. The journal revealed the attitudes of many Americans toward the recently liberated blacks and Canon Benoît's gradual acceptance of the same mentality. The following is an account of his visit to Mobile.

I met at the station Fr. Parishé, S.J., who was born in Naples, 1817. He was Provincial when Bishop O'Connor[1] bought St. Francis Xavier at Baltimore. He foresaw that special exertions would have to be made for the Negroes by the end of the war and therefore encouraged Bishop O'Connor in his work for the colored people. He feared that Archbishop Perché would give no encouragement to St. Joseph's Society, because at the last Plenary Council[2] he spoke strenuously against any special work for the Negroes, since the Negroes themselves preferred to keep their inferior condition among the whites rather than to be an exclusively black congregation.

It has been stated several times elsewhere that the Negroes certainly do not wish to be taught by colored people and on this account, it is said, the Negro Sisters of Baltimore will not succeed. Bishop Gross, however, is forming Negro nuns being convinced that they will prove the best teachers knowing best the foibles of their own race. All admit that a Negro priest would find no favor with his race. . . .

Father Parishé thinks it is the blood and not the climate that makes the Negro. For the Negro who has no white blood in him, is as black as his great, great grand-father; and even the one who has white blood to however large quantity, always retains a little black blood and the smell that ever accompanies it. A student boasted of being of Indian blood. An old Indian, who was told to examine him, set about rubbing his spine between the shoulder blades and soon pronounced him not an Indian, but a Negro by descent. This caused his removal from College.

Later on his trip up the Mississippi River, he had the following conversation with the riverboat captain.

Captain Leathers, the owner of the "Natchez" is a tall, (6 ft.3) and strong built of about 55 years. As he came to chat with me I told him that the object of my voyage was to see the condition of the Negro with a view of

---

1. Bishop Michael O'Connor, S.J. (1820–72), was the first bishop of Pittsburgh and the spiritual director of St. Katherine Drexel. He was responsible for helping the Mill Hill Fathers to come to Baltimore.

2. It is not clear what plenary council this is. Perché was not a bishop at the Second Plenary Council of Baltimore in 1866. At this discussion in the Second Plenary Council, the archbishop of New Orleans, Jean Marie Odin, showed very little enthusiasm for this nationwide effort on behalf of the freed slaves.

working for him. He turned his head away and I could see that this object was to him distasteful and Quixotic. He seemed much relieved by my asking him what he thought about it. For this allowed him at once to speak out his mind, since he was asked without any breach of the civility due to a stranger.

Well, he said, your object is a most useless one. It is a sheer loss of time and money to attempt anything for the Negro. I know him well, having been brought up among the blacks and even I like him: for he is simple and docile. But as for doing anything to raise him above what he is now, is lost labor. God Almighty has made him what he is and you cannot change God's work. He has scarcely any brains, he is a thief, a liar, and not virtuous. If left to himself he would go back to the most loathsome fetichism; he ought to have remained in Africa; he cannot compete with the white man and he will die out in time....

"Diary of a Trip to America, January 6, 1875 to June 8, 1875," by Canon Peter L. Benoit, 3 vols., Mill Hill Fathers Archives, CB6-CB7-CB8, typewritten transcript, CB7-172, 173, 174, and CB7-200, 201, with permission.

Part 5

THE SOUND OF
BLACK CATHOLIC VOICES

30. John R. Slattery, S.S.J., and the Education of Black Priests, 1899

As mentioned above, the Mill Hill Fathers arrived in 1871 in the United States to work among the African American population. By 1893, the American province had broken all ties with Mill Hill and had become independent as the Society of St. Joseph of the Sacred Heart with Cardinal Gibbons, the archbishop of Baltimore, as the superior. John R. Slattery by this time had become more and more convinced of the need for black priests. The following article, which first appeared in Catholic World *in 1899, was the year in which the St. Joseph's College for Negro Catechists at Montgomery, Alabama, opened. The situation of black seminarians at the Josephites' seminary at Epiphany College was uncertain. As a result Slattery hoped by establishing a school to train black catechists — that is, laymen who would perform ministry in black parishes — he would also attract young black men who would be prepared to enter a seminary for priesthood. Unfortunately, Slattery's plans for a future seminary for black students never materialized. After his own defection from the priesthood in 1902, the college never developed into a seminary and remained a sort of high school until its closing in 1922. This article expresses Slattery's unremitting struggle for the education of black priests despite the fact that many of the clergy, including many Josephites, for a variety of reasons were opposed to the ordination of African American men.*

St. Joseph's Society for Negro Missions now numbers twenty-one priests, who labor in seven states:...At present St. Joseph's Seminary has thirty-one divinity students on its roll, and its feeder, the Epiphany Apostolic College, over sixty students....With the spread of missions a new departure has become necessary for the missioners, arising from the need of helpers who will live in the various missions and take, as far as possible, the place of the missionaries while absent. In a word, Catechists, officially and publicly appointed, are now in demand. To understand this let us recall the

RELIGIOUS STATUS OF THE NEGRO RACE.

Of this people 144,536 are given as Catholics in the official report for 1898 of the venerable Commission in charge of the Negro and Indian Fund. This is a very small percentage indeed of eight million American blacks. On the other hand, the various Protestant sects in their official reports claim less than four millions. "Of the eight millions in this country a very large proportion belong to Christian churches; one million six hundred thousand are reported to be members of Baptist churches, about the same number are enrolled in the Methodist churches, and besides these there are Presbyterians, Congregationalists, Episcopalians, and others" (*Negro in America*, by Thomas J. Morgan, D.D.). Hence, four millions may be looked upon as beyond the pale of any religious denomination. Furthermore, in the South Negro Catholics, like white Catholics are bunched, if we may use the term.

Maryland (Diocese of Baltimore) has	37,000	Negro Catholics.	
Louisiana (New Orleans and Natchitoches) has	83,000	"	"
Kentucky (Louisville) has	6,000	"	"
Alabama (Mobile) has	3,425	"	"
In these four States,	129,425	"	"

In other words, Louisiana has more than one-half the Negro Catholics in the United States, and Maryland more than one fourth, both together six-sevenths of them. That is to say, of every seven Negro Catholics in this country four live in Louisiana and two in Maryland. Thus there are left a trifle over 12,000 Catholic Negroes in the other Southern States, and 3,000 in the Bahama Islands (Diocese of New York), which belong to Great Britain.

Again, it is noteworthy that the States in which Negroes are most numerous are the very ones having the fewest Catholics of that race....

To reach these millions, as yet alien even to the sight or voice of a priest, is the work appointed St. Joseph's Society for Colored Missions. It is of the true nature of the apostolic vocation to make use of the people themselves for whom the vocation is divinely granted. As the farmer needs the earth, the astronomer the heavens, the sailor the sea, so does the missionary demand the people, the Josephite the Negro. But quite unlike the earth or sky or waves are the Negroes. For men are they, able to co-operate, not alone by their presence and submissiveness, but also by their action in personally working with the missioners as well as in their influence over their fellows.

NEED OF NEGRO WORKERS ON THE MISSIONS.

No wonder, then, that the common experience of the missionaries of St. Joseph's Society proves that to win and convert the Negroes an indispensable means are the blacks themselves. Appeals, therefore, have come to St. Joseph's Seminary from different fields of labor, urging that Negroes should be trained for the work both as priests and catechists. Now, from their foundation, St. Joseph's Seminary and its feeder, the Epiphany Apostolic College, have had as students Negro boys as well as whites in preparation for the apostolic priesthood to labor among the blacks. At present there are three Negroes in the seminary, and four more in the college. The colored boys, very few in number, are at once introduced among a disproportionate number of whites. Some of them rise to the occasion and equal and even outrank the whites, [for example] two of four Negro seminarians won the A.M. at St. Mary's Seminary, of whom one carried off prizes in both years of philosophy, gaining eight out of ten all round in his studies.

The College for Catechists now under review will tend to increase the number of priestly vocations among Negro youths, although primarily intended to establish a system of Negro catechists. Moreover by its means the bulk of the Negro youths will be trained apart. In this matter we have before us the example of the Protestant sects, which, although throwing open their universities and colleges to the Negro race, have, however, almost all their Negro students in separate institutes....

OBJECT AND METHOD OF TRAINING NEGROES.

It is, in part, to keep alive the faith among our Catholic Negroes, scattered up and down, here and there, like the few grapes left on the vines after the vintage. It is, however, chiefly to meet and offset the influence among Negroes generally of the Protestant Negro preachers and elders, class-leaders and exhorters, that we need Negro catechists, who should be solidly grounded in Christian doctrine and morals and thoroughly trained in a good course of studies. The influence of the Protestant Negro clergy over their church members and people generally should not be pooh-poohed or set down as trivial. The priests in the Negro missions have too often felt its strength. And we were not surprised to receive urgent appeals from our missionaries in five different dioceses urging that this long thought-of college for Negro catechists be started....

Those of the catechists on the mission who persevere will be advanced step by step to the priesthood, while they who marry may remain as catechists. Mission schools will also be taught by these catechists.

Unless fortified by Negro catechists and Negro priests, we shall always be at a disadvantage in dealing with the Negro millions beyond the pale of Holy Church. The Negro looks with suspicion upon white men. The impression left from slavery; the many dishonest tricks upon them; unpaid wages; "store pay"; bad titles to land; unjust mortgages upon their crops; prisoners' stockades — these and countless other wrongs make the Negroes suspicious of the whites. During two-and-twenty years we have been in the closest relations with the black race, have had their confidence in countless ways, are now steadily consulted by them in their little troubles, financial and otherwise; yet we are not afraid to say there is no white man living has a Negro's full confidence....

John R. Slattery, *Catholic World* 70 (1899): 1–3, 9–11.

31. The Trials of a Black Priest, John Henry Dorsey, S.S.J., to John R. Slattery, S.S.J., 1903

John Henry Dorsey was the second black Josephite to be ordained a priest, in 1902 in Baltimore. He was the sixth black priest in American Catholic history. Dorsey was an imposing and impressive preacher. In the beginning of his priesthood, he was a very successful preacher of missions to black Catholic congregations. Nevertheless, his own success raised opposition on the part of many white clergy and white laity. He was not welcomed in all dioceses. Slattery wished Dorsey to go to the College of St. Joseph for catechists. Dorsey did not wish to go, but ultimately accepted the mission. The rector of St. Joseph's College, Thomas Donovan, was not well disposed to Dorsey.

March 21st, 1903

Very Rev. J. R. Slattery
Baltimore, Md.

Reverend and dear Father,

Your letters are at hand. The first seems to censure me for remaining away from Montgomery for so long a time. I wish to say that I had absolutely nothing to do with it. You placed me under Father Donovan and I followed his instructions. In the second you write "do your best, you have a hard life ahead of you." Indeed I realized this before I became a priest and I was determined to suffer for my poor down-trodden people. You also write *"sursum"*[1] and again, "pitch in." I would ask how can one put heart and soul in his work when he knows full well from authentic sources that

---

1. A Latin word meaning "lift up." Taken from the Mass in which the priest calls the people to "lift up your hearts," that is *sursum corda*.

he is *persona non grata*?[2] This thought takes all the energy out of soul and body and leaves a poor frail piece of humanity unfit for anything. When Bishop and priests, from whom encouragement ought to come, oppose themselves to a priest coming into a diocese how can he "pitch in" and do his best. We are human and cannot stop the flood of thought that rushes in upon us. Do not understand from this writing that I am dissatisfied or objecting to your appointment. I have promised obedience and I intend to keep it.

My southern trip was most delightful; although full of hard work my efforts were fully appreciated, and yet there hung over me a dark cloud like the sword over Damocles for I know that I was not wanted in Montgomery, the mission to which you appointed me. I am ready, Rev. Father, to sacrifice all that life holds dear. I have suffered and am willing to endure more. With you I am convinced that the conversion of the colored people will be accomplished by colored priests only. Everything points in that direction.

Catholic Louisiana is losing our people (I mean intelligent colored people) in large numbers every year and there is none coming into the fold. The outlook is very discouraging. I know that the white laity are not opposed to a colored man being raised to the dignity of the priesthood; but on the other hand, in certain localities the priests are; although I must confess that I have been well received by the clergy everywhere even receiving invitations to dine with them.

Do not drive the energy out of man who is willing to do all in his power. Do not kill the fruit in the flower, kill not the oak in the acorn.[3] I have placed my destiny in your hands. Do what you think is best, I bow in humble submission. Kindly remember me to the Fathers and students.

> Wishing you every blessing and begging a prayer for myself.
> I remain your son in Christ,
> John H. Dorsey.

Father Slattery responded to Dorsey's letter a week later. Despite his words to Father Dorsey, Slattery would eventually resign as superior general, leave the Josephites, and eventually leave the Catholic Church.

---

2. A prominent white pastor in Montgomery sought to block Dorsey's coming to St. Joseph College. See Stephen J. Ochs, *Desegregating the Altar: The Josephites and the Struggle for Black Priests, 1871–1960* (Baton Rouge: Louisiana State University Press, 1990), 144–47.

3. Dorsey underlined these sentences.

St. Joseph's Seminary Baltimore Md. Mch. 27th 03

Dear Harry:-

Thank you for your noble letter. No doubt the opposition you will feel keenly, and it depends very much upon yourself to soften it. You must "play possum," do your duty and pay no attention to the outsiders. This is why I am convinced that you will do your best work at the Catechist College. Every graduate stands for a large number, whom you will reach through him. We all suffer from Race prejudice, myself just as much as you. Time and patience and silence are good friends.

Yours sincerely

J. R. Slattery

Dorsey to Slattery, March 21st, 1903, and Slattery to Dorsey, March 27th, 1903, 23-M-42 and 23-M-43, Josephite Archives, Baltimore, with permission.

32. Black Parishioners Write to Their Bishop, 1888

St. Peter's Parish in Charleston, South Carolina, was one of the first black parishes in the United States. It was founded in 1867, shortly after the Civil War, by Bishop Lynch. It had a board of trustees with James Spencer, an important figure in the Black Catholic Congresses, as the secretary. The trustees gave evidence of an independent spirit.

Charlestown, S.C. April 21, 1888.

Right Reverend H. P. Northrop, bishop of Charleston, S.C.

As faithful children of God and humble and devoted members of the Roman Catholic Church, who are desirous to do at all times that which is right and most pleasing in the sight of God our Savior and which only can be done by strict compliance with the law of His Most Holy Church, which He has commanded us to hear. We the undersigned members of St. Peter's Church and representatives of the said Congregation, having heard the reading of the "Circular Letter" which by your authority was read in the several Catholic Churches on Sunday last in which you advise and request the white Catholics of the respective churches to attend services and confine themselves to their own parish churches in the future and thus avoid any interference with the congregation of St. Peter's.

In order therefore that we may understand more definitely the interpretation of your letter and at the same time that we may know exactly our position, and what will be required of us in the Church at a special meeting held on the above date it was unanimously adopted the following resolution.

Resolved that we the undersigned members of St. Peter's for our own information and satisfaction, respectfully submit the following question, *viz.*,

First. Are we to understand by the Circular Letter that no white Catholics whether living in the parish of St. Peter's or not shall attend Holy Mass at this Church?

Second. Are those Colored Catholics living far away from St. Peter's Church and in other parishes, expected and required to attend services at St. Peter's notwithstanding the fact that there are a great many who live in other parishes who are infirm, aged and otherwise afflicted?

Third. Are we the Colored Catholics of the City to be excluded from attending divine services at the other Catholic Churches or will we be protected and welcomed should we present ourselves at the other Churches for the purpose of complying with the precepts of the Church?

These questions are asked because to us as a Congregation they are important in as much as we have been specially mentioned and noticed in your "Circular" and for this reason we have as humble and faithful members of the Roman Catholic Church, submitted the same to you our Pastor and ask for information in order that we may know something of our future position and obligations in the Church to which we are firmly united.

With much respect, I have the honor to remain

Very respectfully Yours etc.

Jas. A. Spencer, Sec. of the Meeting.

Signed.

E. L. Boisdon.	Thos. M. Holmes.	Jos. P. Guenveur.	F. M. David	M. P. Carroll.
A. Chaponie.	C. D. Hayne.	E. M. Castion.	Jno. F. Peronneau	T. L. Castion.
R. K. Harrison.	W. H. Myers.	W. H. Logan.	Jos. Ash. C. J. Jones	A. J. Castion.
	Thos. Bergman.		O. F. Castion.	

Bishop Northrop responded in the following letter.

Episcopal Residence. 114 Broad Street
Charlestown, S.C. May 3d 1888.

Mr James Spencer and others,

Dear Sirs,

Your very respectful and loyal address and Resolutions were on my desk when I returned from a visit to North Carolina on Saturday last. I read it with great pleasure, but have been so engaged since my return that I have had scarcely a chance to acknowledge it as I now do. I do not propose to answer or explain or write a word on the subject matter laid before me but to invite you and the other gentlemen who have signed this document and any other members (male of course) of the Congregation of St. Peters to meet me at my residence No. 114 Broad Street at any hour convenient to them. I would suggest to save time, that you meet me here to-morrow evening (Friday 4th) at 9 or 9:30 P.M. so that we can discuss as bretheren should do or as a father (though most unworthy) with his children the very important and absorbing interest in which we all are so much concerned. Praying that the Holy Ghost may direct and guide us all

> Very sincerely in Christ,
> H. P. Northrop,
> Bp. of Charleston, S.C.

2-R-1i, 2-R-1j, 2-R-1k, Josephite Archives, Baltimore, with permission.

33. Daniel Rudd, Newspaper Editor, Lecturer, Lay Leader, 1888

Daniel Rudd (1854–1933), born in Bardstown, Kentucky, edited a black Catholic newspaper in Cincinnati and later in Detroit. Convinced of the Catholic Church's ability to bring about a change in the situation of American blacks and convinced that there would be a future mass conversion of blacks, Rudd used the newspaper to bring about a series of African American Catholic lay congresses. The following articles from his weekly newspaper express his convictions and his plans for the Black Catholic Congresses. In one editorial, Rudd gave the following account of his talk to the Catholic Young Men's National Union in Cincinnati.

The meeting of the Catholic Young Men's National Union, has already received extensive notice in these columns, but as our space was limited we were compelled to leave out much that is of vital importance to the Colored people. We have already stated that a mention of the proposed congress of Colored Catholics of the U.S., met with an approval that spoke in no uncertain tones. We now present our readers with the speech of the editor of this paper and the resolution passed at its close, as copied from the minutes of the convention....

Mr Rudd: ...I hardly expected when at my home a little boy, in the State of Kentucky, that at this early day of my life—and I am a young man yet—I would be standing before a Catholic Convention of this Union, to lift my voice in the interest of my race and of my Church, but such is the case....It may seem strange to you, possibly as Catholics to hear me talking about Colored Catholics, or any other sort of Catholics, yet it must be so; we have in this country a large number of our own race, many of whom are Catholics, more possibly than any one of you have ever imagined, various estimates have been given, but for our own purpose, we prefer to give our

Daniel Rudd (1854–1933). Journalist, lecturer, convenor of the first Black Catholic Congress, 1889 (souvenir volume of the centennial celebration and Catholic Congress, 1789–1889 [Detroit: William H. Hughes, Publisher, 1889], 21).

own figures. I believe that there are about two hundred thousand practical Catholics in the United States of my race. [Applause].

That is, indeed, a grand showing, considering, if you please, that we have done nothing ourselves to promote and facilitate a knowledge of the Church among our own race, except possibly to attend to our own duties, and thought that we were doing well, if we succeeded in keeping ourselves in line individually. According to the statistics there are seven millions of Negroes in the United States. My friends, this race is increasing more rapidly than yours, and if it continues to increase in the future as it has in the past, by the middle of the next century they will outnumber your race. This is worthy of your consideration.

There are a good many things going on within my own race that I do not know anything about, but this I do know; We seek to place all citizens upon the basis that the law says they should stand, they stand alike in the Catholic Church, in the glory and grandeur of her history, she has been impartial. We turn to her and ask that she shall teach men a decent respect for God and each other. [Applause].

There has been a great deal of missinformation [*sic*] among our race, and that is why many more have not been in the Church, for my own part it was a pleasure for me to have been raised a Catholic....We have been led to believe that the Church was inimical to the Negro race, inimical to the genius of our Republic. This is not true, I feel that I owe it to myself, my God, and my country to refute the slander.

We are publishing a weekly newspaper, whatever it is, it is the best we can do in this work. A meeting of our people will be held somewhere, the times and place has not yet been fixed, but I am here, gentlemen, to ask your assistance, to ask your kindness, and you have shown it to me today.

When that convention meets, I trust that many of you will either by your presence, or in some other way show your interest in this work. I believe that within ten years, if the work goes on as it has been going on, there will be awakened a latent force in this country. Possibly you do not know how much has been done in this line. At Baltimore there are three churches, there are two already built and one building, also a convent; in Washington City there is one of the finest churches in this country belonging to the Colored Catholics; in Charleston, S.C., there are two churches; in Kansas City, colored sisters have taken hold; in New Orleans there is a church. In this city we have one on New street, small though as it is, its members are at least earnest and good Catholics. [Applause]. We have a seminary in Baltimore, a priest at Quincy, Illinois. We have one out in Louisville, Ky. The Society of St. Joseph is doing a grand work. This is not all but I must stop here....

> *American Catholic Tribune,* June 15, 1888, microfilm, ATLA, in Archives of the
> Archdiocese of Philadelphia, with permission.

34. Daniel Rudd Explains the Proposed Congress of Black Catholics, 1888

Thousands of the subscribers of the *American Catholic Tribune* would no doubt like to know what prompted us to ask that a Congress of Catholics be held in this country....

We had watched for years the tendency on the part of some people to ignore the Negro as a man and citizen in the United States. We had noted the progress from other parts of the earth. We had seen that although our race had spent two and a half centuries here laboring without pay, when civilization had become civilized enough to let us walk about the country, our race had served so long, so faithfully, and received only kicks and robbery for reward, the robber spirit of caste discrimination, the crop-mortgage system, the prison labor lease system, the unequal tax system, all kindred evils, remnants of a barbarous past, still stood Gibraltar like to bar our advancement; we thought that if we would turn the attention of our people to the moral truths and the exact equality of the human family before God, as taught by Holy Mother Church Universal that spouse of Christ our Lord would lift us as she has the mighty Caucassian [*sic*] race from oppression, doubt, ignorance, and place on a higher plane of moral and intellectual life. To prove that although the Negro is submissive he is neither a coward nor an ingrate, we appeal to the written pages of impartial history. To prove that the Negro is capable of the highest moral and intellectual culture we point not only to the thousands who now sleep their last sleep having left good deeds to tell of them, but also point with pride to a Tolton, a Douglass, a Reason, to the Oblate Sisters of Providence, all grand good people in their respective callings of life as well as to thousands of others who have advanced step by step until to-day the Negro is found in "every avenue of life in which the energy of man avails to conquer" and that too in the face of prejudice and discrimination.

"Knowing that he who would be free must himself strike the blow," we thought the best way to turn the attention of our race to Church was first find out how many Catholics we would have to start with and then put that force to work. Acting on this we spent nearly two years in traveling over the Northern, Eastern, and Southern portion of our country to see for ourselves something of the material with which we would have to start and telling our friends what we wanted to do. The result of the work is most gratifying. We not only found thousands of scholarly and wealthy Negro Catholics who stood ready to work for the race and church but we have been able to enlist the zeal of that matchless army of Christian workers — the bishops and clergy of the Church. In addition to this, recent conversion to the faith show that our force is not yet measured. Thompson, Ruffin and a number of others are recent conversions, and they are men of culture and high moral standing. The Catholic press and laity now lift a voice that will be heard around the earth. Our figures are 200,000 Colored Catholics to begin with and we are sure that a Congress fairly representing this large number of people will be of great interest and advantage to the race but will be an honor to the Church. Hence the call which is now being prepared will soon be issued.

American Catholic Tribune, June 22, 1888, with permission.

35. Daniel Rudd's Two Letters to William Henry Elder, Archbishop of Cincinnati, 1888

Rudd received many forms of assistance from William Henry Elder, the archbishop of Cincinnati. In the following letter, Rudd acknowledged the assistance Elder gave to the publication of the American Catholic Tribune; *in the second letter, Rudd acknowledged the support that the archbishop had given him in traveling to Europe to meet Cardinal Lavigerie, the renowned apostle to Africa, and be present at the antislavery conference organized by him. Rudd discovered that the congress was postponed when he had already arrived in Germany. Nonetheless, Rudd was able to write Elder about his visit with Lavigerie and with Cardinal Manning, the archbishop of Westminster.*

Boston, May 3rd 1888.

Most Rev. Wm Henry Elder,
Dear Archbishop:

We have every reason to thank you for your kindness to us and to American Catholic Tribune for it was by your approval that the paper was able to stem the tide for that most dangerous period of the life of any newspaper, the first year. It was your approval also that gave us standing among the prelates and clergy of this country. We will seek to maintain and improve the paper in the future. It will be enlarged to an 8 column about the middle of next month. We will also by that time be able to devote our entire time and attention to it [*sic*] literary and mechanical makeup.

Hoping that we may continue to merit your kind approval and praying your blessing I am yours obediently,

Dan. A. Rudd

Daniel A. Rudd, May 3, 7, and 25, 1888, Archives of the Archdiocese of Cincinnati, with permission.

London Aug. 12th 1889.

Most Rev. Dear Sir: — When I arrived in Hamburg, I saw in one of the German papers, a dispatch dated July 24th, saying that the Congress had been indefinitely postponed. I continued, however to Lucerne, arriving there August 3rd. The dispatch proved to be correct. I did not see His Eminence until the 5th as he was at Ochenstein and only arrived Sunday night August 4th.

I met Mr. Ruffin of Boston at the Cardinal's residence. The reception extended us was royal, for His Eminence kissed us like a father. So overjoyed was Africa's great Apostle when he read our letters and credentials that he said our very presence there would give him new life and new zeal to work for a race that is so full of gratitude. Thinking I would get home as soon as a letter, I did not write you. I stopped two days in Paris and am now in London, where I shall remain until August 20th, at the invitation of His Eminence Cardinal Manning to whom I had a word of introduction by Cardinal Lavigerie.

We were invited to address a large meeting at St. George's Cathedral Hall last night and those who were present there seemed delighted at what was said. I will be home about the first of September.

I bear an appointment from Cardinal Lavigerie, as the American Correspondent and representative of his work for the African Slaves.

With kind regards for those who may enquire of me, I am Obediently yours

Dan. A. Rudd

Most Rev. W. H. Elder
Archbishop Cincinnati

P.S. We are invited by His Eminence Cardinal Manning to accompany him in his carriage to the annual meeting of the League of the Cross at Crystal Palace next Monday. Dan.

> Daniel Rudd, August 12 and 26, 1889, Archives of the Archdiocese of Cincinnati, with permission.

36. The Black Catholic Lay Congresses, 1889, 1893

There were five Black Catholic Congresses, beginning in 1889 until 1894. It seems that the delegates were all men. The first congress was held in Washington, D.C., in January 1889. The fourth was held in Chicago in 1893, in conjunction with the Columbian Exposition. These congresses are an important source for the mentality and attitudes of black Catholic laypeople at a time when they were almost ignored by the white majority. These ideas were often summed up in a closing message to their fellow Catholics. The following are excerpts from the closing address of the first Black Catholic Congress in 1889, and the second is from the closing address of the fourth Black Catholic Congress in 1893.

Address of the Congress to Their Catholic Fellow Citizens of the United States, 1889

Assembled in capital of our country, on the opening of the year 1889, in the presence and under the patronage of his Eminence Cardinal Gibbons,

Archbishop of Baltimore, and with the approval of our Catholic hierarchy we delegates of the Colored Catholics of the United States, deem it proper, at the close of the deliberations, to address our Fellow Catholic citizens of this country, and to put before them a summary of the work we have accomplished.

Several hundred in number, gathered from the various States of the Union — from the Mississippi to the Atlantic, from the Great Lakes to the Gulf — we opened our convention with Solemn Mass, of which the celebrant was the Rev. Augustus Tolton, our trusted and worthy brother in race as in creed, in whose elevation to the priesthood we rejoice, and in the presence of Cardinal Gibbons, who graciously condescended to be with us, and who, by his words of encouragement stimulated our efforts.

In this meeting, even under such encouraging patronage, to consider, in a public manner and for the first time in our history the needs and claims of our race, it was natural to feel that a hurculean [sic] task awaited us. But, relying on the assistance of the Holy Ghost, whose inspiration, we have no doubt prompted the call of this assembly ... and encouraged in our labors by the beautiful spectacle of nearly two hundred intelligent and Christian men, representing every section of this vast country, we congratulate ourselves upon the results at which we have arrived.

Although we did not, at the outset, presume to think that this Congress could be other than an humble experiment — although we do not, even still, presume to claim that its results be other than an entering wedge in the breaking of the mighty wall of difficulties lifted up for centuries against us and a mere preliminary step in the progressive march and final regeneration of our people — yet we feel that we can safely present these results to the entire world, assured that they will mark the dawn of a new and brighter era in the history of our race in every land wherein it is established.

While we may well rejoice over the progress made by our Colored fellow-citizens within the last quarter of a century, since they have been permitted to enjoy, to some extent, the inalienable rights given to every man in the very dawn of creation, we must admit — only to lament it — the fact that the sacred rights of justice and of humanity are still sadly wounded — are still immeasurably obstructed — even in a country where liberty, so long an exile, so long abused, so long a wanderer the world over has found at last a secure refuge, a permanent home, a grand and lasting temple.

Knowing too well, however, that time alone, accompanied and overshadowed by the providential shaping of an all wise God, will eventually remove such obstructions. Knowing, too that our divinely established and divinely guided Church, ever the true friend of the down trodden, will, by the innate force of her truth, gradually dispel the prejudices unhappily prevailing amongst so many of our misguided people, and therefore, anxious not to forestall in any way the time marked by God for bringing about this great work, we feel confident that this solemn expression of our convictions, of our hopes and of our resolutions, will have at least the advantage of proving that we — the Catholic representatives of our people — have earnestly contributed our humble share to the great work for whose final accomplishment all our brothers are ardently yearning.

The education of a people being the great and fundamental means of elevating it to the higher planes to which all Christian civilization tends, we pledge ourselves to aid in establishing, wherever we are to be found, Catholic schools, embracing the primary and higher branches of knowledge, as in them and through them alone can we expect to reach the large masses of Colored children now growing up in the country without a semblance of Christian education....

> "Proceedings of the First Colored Catholic Congress Held in Washington, D.C., January 1, 2 and 3, 1889," in *Three Catholic Afro-American Congresses* (New York: Arno Press, 1978) [*The American Catholic Tradition* (Cincinnati: American Catholic Tribune, 1898), 66–69], with permission.

The Fourth Black Catholic Congress, Chicago, 1893

The Colored Catholics of the United States, through their representatives to the fourth congress in convention assembled in the city of Chicago.... We first renew our profession of love and loyalty to the Holy Church and our submission to the See at Rome. We congratulate our fellow Catholics and ourselves on the manifestation of the solicitude of love of Pope Leo XIII in behalf of the members of the Church in the United States in the appointment of His Excellency Monsignor Satolli as Apostolic Delegate.

The Catholic Church, guided by the spirit of truth, must always preserve inviolate the deposit of faith, and thus she cannot err in proclaiming the rights of man.... From the day of Christ it has been her mission to inculcate the doctrine of love, and not of hate; to raise up the downtrodden, and to rebuke the proud. It has been her mission to proclaim to the ends of the earth that we all have stamped on our immortal souls the image of God, that by baptism we have become the brethren of Jesus Christ, and made heirs of one blessed home of everlasting happiness. For ages the Church has labored to break down the walls of race prejudice, to teach the world the doctrine of the meek and humble Christ, that man should be gauged by his moral worth; that virtue alone, springing from grace, truly elevates a man, and that vice alone, springing from the malice of the heart, degrades him. Though the practice of the Church is consistent with her divine doctrine, we must deplore the fact that some of her members in various parts of the country have, in the words of our very distinguished friend, the Most Rev. John Ireland, "departed from the teaching of the Church in the treatment of the colored Catholics and yielded right to popular prejudice." As children of the true Church, we are anxious to witness the extension of our beloved religion among those of our brethren who as yet are not blessed with the true Faith, and therefore we consider it a duty, not only to ourselves but to the Church and to God, that we draw the attention of every member of the learned Roman hierarchy to such violations from Catholic law and Catholic practice....

A distinguished lady of color, who is not a Catholic, asserts that the Catholic Church, of all Christian Churches, comes nearest to practicing the doctrines of the rights of man. We know that the Roman Church, as she is One and Apostolic, is also Catholic and Holy. With thorough confidence in the rectitude of our course in the enduring love of Mother Church, and the consciousness of our priesthood, we show our devotion to the Church, our jealousy of her glory and our love for her history in that we respectfully call the attention of the Catholic world, and in particular of the clergy, to those wrong practices which mark the conduct of those of the clergy who have yielded to the popular prejudice. Instances of such weakness, though not numerous, are still not so rare but that a remedy should be applied. Those who have departed from the teachings of the Church we would see reclaimed, and those of our own people who have not yet had their eyes opened to the light of God we would see converted.

In the name of our brethren throughout America, we desire to thank the Church for the many charities conducted, North and South, by Catholic philanthropy, distinctly for our people. We heartily endorse the magnificent effort our Church is making in educating our youth on industrial lines. We are proud of our parochial schools, our orphanages and higher educational institutions; but above all things, we rejoice that our Church, the Church of our love, the Church of our faith, has not failed to stand by its historic record.

For did not the Holy Church canonize Augustine and Monica, Benedict the Moor, Cyprian, and Cyril, Perpetua and Felicity [text corrected]? And, at this time, notwithstanding race antagonism is at its height, notwithstanding, after only thirty years of freedom, the Negro is a man and brother, public opinion has molded the sentiment that a Negro could not be a priest of the Roman Catholic Church. The Catholic Church has rebuked this settlement[1] by ordaining the Rev. Father A. Tolton, the first Negro priest in America, and the Rev. C. R. Uncles to the exalted estate of Catholic priesthood. We desire to say every encouragement, every fraternal greeting extended the priests of our race, are in our opinion so many more proofs of the Divine truth of Catholic religion. The Catholic spirit we ask for in the future is that exemplified by the Columbian Catholic Congress in making the Colored Catholic Congress a part of itself.

In conclusion we say in all sincerity that, should the clergy, where rests their responsibility, see to it that in all instances and in all places the truth of Catholic doctrine, which knows no distinction of races or previous condition, be maintained, the day will yet come when the whole colored race of the United States will be knocking at her doors for admittance, anxious to be of that faith which teaches and practices the sublime essence of human rights in the sight of God and our fellow man.

Respectfully,

L. C. Vallé, Illinois
Fred L. McGhee, Minnesota
R. N. Woods, New York
S. K. Govern, Pennsylvania
C. H. Butler, District of Columbia
Daniel Rudd, Ohio
W. J. Smith, District of Columbia
William K. Easton, Texas, Chairman

Text published in Cyprian Davis, O.S.B., "Two Sides of a Coin: The Black Presence in the History of the Catholic Church in America," in *Many Rains Ago: A Historical Theological Reflection on the Role of the Episcopate in the Evangelization of African American Catholics* (Washington, D.C.: Secretariat for Black Catholics, USCC/NCCB, 1990), 57–58, with permission.

37. Charles H. Butler of Washington, D.C., "The Condition and Future of the Negro Race," 1893

The Columbian Catholic Congress took place at the same time as the Fourth Black Catholic Congress. The two congresses met separately, but a member of the Columbian Catholic Congress moved that the delegates of the Black Catholic Congress should join them at one session. At this session Charles Butler, a delegate of the Black Catholic Congress from Washington, D.C., read the following paper. Let it be noted that Butler was in agreement

---

1. Read "sentiment." [Ed.]

with Booker T. Washington regarding the position of blacks socializing with whites.

What shall I say of the future of the negro race in the United States? His future depends upon his treatment to a great measure by the white man; whether the proud Anglo-Saxon intends to dispossess himself of mere race prejudice and accord his black brother simple justice. If continual warfare is to be carried on against him because of the accident of color, then all his efforts are in vain. But I am strong to believe that the dust of American prejudice will be cleared from the eyes of our white fellow-citizens, they will learn to discriminate, not by the color of a man's skin, but by the test that all men should adhere to — character and ability. There is one subject upon which the negro has been greatly misunderstood by his Friends and purposely so by his enemies — they have the clear and definite term "civil equality" synonymous with that other definite term of entirely different significance, "social equality." If civil equality and social equality had the same application there would be room for complaint and justly so, but upon a calm and dispassionate thought it must be apparent to all intelligent men that such a thing would be as distasteful to the negro as to the white man. Civil equality makes no such proposal, bears no such result. Public society and civil society comprise one distinct group of mutual relations and private society entirely another, and it is evil to confuse the two....

My voice has been lifted upon many occasions upon this subject of caste prejudice. I have pleaded with all the earnestness of my soul that all the avenues of human activity be opened to the negro race, and that they be given a fair and impartial trial. Will this be done? For upon this rests their case. I can not dismiss this consideration without saying a word to those who would carry their prejudices into the sacred confines of God's holy church, and relegate the negro to an obscure corner of the church, and endeavor to make him feel that he is not as good as the rest of God's creatures for the reason of the accident of color. How long, oh Lord, are we to endure this hardship in the house of our friends?...

Progress of the Catholic Church in America and the Great Columbian Catholic Congress of 1893, 2 vols. in one (Chicago: J. S. Hyland and Co., 1897), 121–25.

Charles H. Butler. Active member of all the Black Catholic Lay Congresses. Address: "The Condition and Future of the Negro Race," September 7, 1893. Reprinted with the permission of Charles B. Cobbs.

Part 6

THE "COLOR LINE" OF THE TWENTIETH CENTURY

38. Letter of Cardinal Gotti to the Apostolic Delegate on the Treatment of Black Catholics, 1904

Girolamo Maria Gotti, O.D.C., became prefect of the Congregation of the Propaganda in 1902. This letter was sent to Archbishop Diomede Falconio, O.F.M., who was apostolic delegate to the United States from 1902 to 1911. The U.S. Catholic Church was under the direction of the Congregation of the Propaganda until 1908.

APOSTOLIC DELEGATION
Washington, D.C.
United States of America

Rome, January 18, 1904

Your Excellency: —

It has been referred to this Sacred Congregation that in some of the Dioceses of the United States, the condition of the Catholic negro, not only in respect to the other faithful, but also in respect to their pastors and Bishops, is very humiliating and entirely different from that of the whites.

As this is not in conformity with the spirit of Christianity which proclaims the equality of all men before God, that equality which foments charity and tends to the increase of Religion by multiplying the number of conversions. I ask Your Excellency to call the attention of His Eminence Cardinal Gibbons to this matter, so that in their next meeting the Most Reverend Archbishops may take the necessary steps to procure that this diversity of treatment may be lessened and thus, little by little entirely removed.

(signed) Fr. C. Card. Gotti., Pref.
Luigi Veccia, segret.

101-G-6, Archives of the Archdiocese of Baltimore, with permission.

39. A Report to the Holy See on the Situation of African Americans in the United States, 1903

Joseph Anciaux was a Belgian who served with the Josephites until he returned to Belgium in 1908, where he died in 1931. Anciaux wrote a scathing report in Latin on the situation of blacks in the United States that was printed in Belgium in 1903. Anciaux sent this report to the Holy See. An English translation of an excerpt of this document is printed below.

Concerning the Wretched Condition Of Negro Catholics in America.
Joseph Anciaux, Missioner of America.

... In many churches Negroes have a narrow or despised place which is called in English, *back-side,* or *gallery;* they cannot enter their own church without undergoing humiliation. Nowhere in the Southern States are Negroes or those who are called *mixed* admitted to Catholic schools with white students. In no college operated by Benedictines, Dominicans, Jesuits, and so forth, are they admitted unless perhaps very recently some Cubans or Filipinos.... In every convent of religious women, a girl having a little Negro blood in her veins is immediately rejected; such a girl will not be admitted under any pretext in a home with white girls, even to prepare for First Communion. It does not matter at all that she is well-educated, pious, pure, and truly Catholic, so long as she seems Negro or there is the slightest suspicion of color.... [A] few months ago when I came to the Cathedral Church of New Orleans I greeted the respected Vicar General, the illustrious [John Marius] Laval[1] and spoke with him in a familiar way about the Negroes. His Reverence is endowed with genius, virtue, and charity, and I have no intention of offending him, but he expressed this astonishing opinion: "In America no Negro should be ordained. Just as illegitimate sons are declared irregular by Canon Law, so, to settle the whole question, the Negroes could be declared irregular because they are held in contempt by white people." And he added: "I offer this as my private opinion, as it were."

Would that it were a private opinion: But it is not only private, but very false and most alien to the mind of the Church! FOR ALWAYS AND EVERY-WHERE THE SUPREME PONTIFFS HAVE FOSTERED WITH THE GREATEST SOLICITUDE THE EDUCATION OF A NATIVE CLERGY.

---

1. John Marius Laval, vicar general, became auxiliary bishop of New Orleans in 1911. He died in 1937. [Ed.]

It should be noted carefully that no reason or even pretext of danger or immorality is invoked by this prelate against the Negroes. His entire feeling is included in these words: "Irregular because Negro."

> "De Miserabili Conditione Catholicorum Nigrorum in America," Josephite Archives, Baltimore, with permission.

40. "The Catholic Church and the Negro," by Lincoln Vallé: The Failure of the Catholic Church in the South to Reach Out to African Americans, 1923

Lincoln Vallé was a collaborator with Daniel Rudd in the Black Catholic Congresses of the 1890s and a correspondent for Rudd's newspaper, The American Catholic Tribune. *Vallé worked in Milwaukee as a lay evangelist in the black community. The article in* America *was in answer to an earlier article about Catholic missionaries working in the South. For Vallé the Church made a major mistake in not reaching out to the members of the black Catholic community who were the natural leaders.*

...In connection with the facts so plainly presented...I wish to add...a few facts showing the reason Catholicism among the Negroes in the South was and is slow. I submit these facts from what I have learned from personal contact and through years of practical experience.

Unfortunately had the Catholic Church in America immediately after the Negro's Emancipation accepted the burden of caring for his welfare, through her commission, her board for work among the colored people and her societies and several diocesan agencies, as she is doing today, the progress of the Negro race would be more permanent. The Catholic Church which possesses the deposit of Divine Faith is the only organism capable of producing, developing and maintaining in the race an adequate, moral basis, necessary for any noteworthy success.

The Negro has always sought a channel for artistic solace, into which he could throw the symbolism of his racial longing. He found it in the religion brought to him by Protestant missionaries or taught him by his masters. Here he was free to dream his dreams and create his visions of future happiness, for no master could punish him for praising God. Thus he "found religion" and in religion he found no mood of his simple soul unnourished.

It would have been easy after the freedom of the Negro to convert him to the Catholic Church. Her music, her vestments, her glorious Te Deums, her canticles would have been a balm to his saddened heart and soul.

It will be news to our fellow-Catholics to learn that there are nearly one hundred Negro schools of higher education scattered throughout the South which are supported by Protestant denominations. The Protestants not only spend money directly for the support of these institutions, but they spend many thousands more among their trained lay forces of Negroes who fill these schools with pupils and assist very considerably in replenishing the funds necessary to the work. Just think of it, 20,000 youths of both sexes enjoying the advantages of high graded education, fitting them for leadership among their race. Yearly, two thousand or more pass from these schools into active life, equipped as school teachers, doctors, lawyers, editors, and preachers, all recognized race leaders, with comparatively few not engaged in active and positive opposition to our Holy Mother Church....These facts bear out the statement made by R. Strong McGregor when he says, "The Negro Catholic movement will never be what it should until we have won a much larger percentage of the leading class to a better disposition towards Catholics."

It is true that the Catholic Church in America has accepted the burden of their care and their welfare, and through her commission, her board for work among colored people...but she is handicapped, not by the inefficiency nor the paucity of workers in the field, but by the general apathy of the white laity....This apathy on the part of the white laity is on account of the absence of the cooperation of a Negro Catholic leadership. It is the play of "Hamlet" with Hamlet left out.

The Negro's innate energy, properly directed, should and must be the energizing force in the race's advance, and it should be given free play. A race when educated, must be its own dynamo. The value of Negro self-aid is well appreciated by our Protestant friends who make much use of the Negroes themselves in all their missionary work among them....

America 30 (1923–24): 327–28.

41. Thomas Wyatt Turner, Black Catholic Lay Leader of the Twentieth Century, a Letter to an Archbishop on the Situation of Black Catholics, 1919, and Letter to the Bishops, 1932

Thomas Wyatt Turner (1877–1978) became the leader of the black Catholic community in the course of the First World War. A fervently loyal Catholic, he fought against the many racist practices within the Catholic Church in the United States. He helped organize a black Catholic movement which eventually became known as the Federated Colored Catholics, somewhat similar to the movement begun by Daniel Rudd at the end of the nineteenth century. Turner was a university professor who believed that black Catholics must organize themselves to work against racial segregation and that they must take responsibility themselves for carrying out this task. Turner believed that black lay Catholics should lead the movement. This brought him into conflict with leaders in the interracial movement such as John LaFarge, S.J., and William Markoe, S.J., as well as with fellow black Catholics who were more accommodating to the ideas of LaFarge and Markoe. The two letters that follow reveal his determined opposition to racial segregation within the Church and the basic purpose of the black Catholic movement which he began.

Most Reverend and dear Sir:

As Catholics who have always been loyal and faithful to Holy Mother Church, we beg to call your attention to the discrimination and handicaps that are intentionally and unjustly placed in the way of the colored Catholics through certain growing practice in the Church.

We feel very strongly that these practices are going exactly contrary to the teachings of our Lord and every tradition of the Church when they discriminate against people because of color, but when these un-christian acts are directed against faithful fellow members of the Church we urgently call upon you to lend the weight of your authority in preventing them.

We desire to call your attention to the pressing need for more colored priests to aid in the work of bringing the colored population into the Church. During the last census period statistics show an increase in those denominations with a large colored ministry of 85 percent, while the increase of colored communicants in such a denomination as ours was only 14 percent. This is certainly food for thought. We feel that there are ample facilities existing at present for education of such clergy at Joseph's seminary,[1] and we beg to inquire why this society has adopted a policy against admitting colored candidates for the priesthood.

We beg further to call your attention to the uncalled for new policy of refusing Catholic colored boys at the Catholic University. This act is without justification or cause and is another manifestation of the unchecked growth of race prejudice in the Church.

The elementary and high school facilities offered our children by the Church have been very scant and falls [*sic*] far below those offered by any other denomination. The M.E. [Methodist Episcopal] Church is now preparing to spend $6,000,000 and the Presbyterian Church $400,000 on the education of the Negro.

We further ask representation for the Catholic colored layman on all boards of the Church planning his welfare, for we do not feel that adequate opinion of the needs and necessities of the Negro can be received from any one except the Negro himself.

---

1. The Josephite Seminary in Baltimore. [Ed.]

In parishes where there is a mixed congregation, the Priest continuously urge [*sic*] the sending of children to Catholic schools. No Catholic colored child is admitted, but they do admit white Protestant children. And this, too, in view of the fact that the colored members of the congregation gave substantial financial support in erecting such schools and are expected, and do, contribute to the support and maintenance of the same.

Very faithfully yours

The papers of Thomas Wyatt Turner, TWT-21, United States Catholic Conference Archives, Washington, D.C., with permission.

November 14, 1932

To the American Hierarchy
Washington, D.C.

Your Eminences and Your Excellencies:

In compliance with the instructions received from the Most Reverend Emmett M. Walsh, D.C., Secretary of the Meeting of the Hierarchy, dated, November 13, 1931, the Federated Colored Catholics of the United States have prepared a statement of the things that colored Catholics wish to have done to advance the true religion in their own lives and to so present our holy faith to all non-Catholic colored people that the Church may win them for Christ.

We hope to arrange to have this statement brought before the annual meeting of the Hierarchy this Fall, but we are sending you this copy so that you may give it consideration before the time for action arrives.

Encouraged by the consideration that was given to our appeal last Fall, we look to our Hierarchy for such action as is necessary to repair the rent in the seamless garment of Christ, to remove the sad division that exists in the otherwise glorious Catholic Church in this country.

Colored Catholics ask of the bishops of the country that every bishop in his own diocese shall take such steps as are necessary to remove and to prevent any rulings coming from the clergy or from religious which would deny them the same practice of all activities of their religion that is accorded to white Catholics.

They ask that in sections of the country where civil law limits the complete fulfilment of the above; the bishops and the clergy work earnestly for the repeal of all statutes limiting the full and free exercise of their religion; and that bishops and clergy enlist the help of influential white laymen in securing the repeal of such statutes.

They ask that every bishop shall see to it that no Catholic institution in his diocese, school; hospital; protectory; orphanage; college; university; or

Thomas Wyatt Turner (1877–1978). Black Catholic lay leader of the twentieth century. Reprinted with the permission of the Archives of the Josephite Fathers, Baltimore.

seminary, shall be closed to colored Catholics because of the color of their skin, and that the bishop shall labor to remove any bar to this that civil law may place.

They ask that every bishop carry on in his diocese a campaign of education; among his clergy, beginning with the students in the seminary; among the Religious, beginning with the postulants and novices.... They ask that the bishop shall see that his priests shall preach to their people that those uncatholic and prejudices [*sic*] actions which make of the colored Catholic someone apart from other Catholics are seriously contrary to that second great commandment; "Thou shalt love thy neighbor as thyself...."

They ask that every bishop strive and plan; and see that his priests and sisters strive and plan to discover and to foster vocations to the priesthood and to the religious life in colored Catholic boys and girls; and that the bishop, priests and teachers give to the cultivation of vocations in colored children at least as great [an] effort as they give to vocations in white children, inasmuch as the vocations of the colored are more needed, and are beset by more and greater obstacles.... They ask that on the occasion of some public and gross outrage of the rights of the colored people in general; whether Catholic or not; such as lynching; the driving out of the colored residents from a town; or the like, that the bishop and the priests take occasion to make public the attitude of the Catholic Church to such injustices....

Respectfully,
Thomas W. Turner
President

N.C.C.B. Office of the General Secretary, Archives, Catholic University of America, with permission.

42. Permission Granted to Found the Franciscan Handmaids of Mary, Savannah, 1916

A third congregation of black sisters was founded in Georgia after the First World War by Ignatius Lissner of the Society of African Missions in 1916. The congregation was founded because there was a danger that the Georgia legislature would outlaw the teaching of black children by white teachers, in this instance white sisters. In the end the legislation was not passed, but by then the community was established with the help of Elizabeth Barbara Williams, who as Mother Theodore Williams moved the community in 1922 from Savannah, Georgia, to Harlem in New York, where, affiliated to the Franciscan Order, the small community of sisters placed themselves in the service of the poor in the African American community.

Bishop Keiley had turned over the African American missions to Father Lissner and the Society of African Missions. In time a violent dispute would arise between Lissner and Bishop Keiley. Keiley had great interest in the evangelization of African Americans. At the same time, he found it difficult to accept absolute equality between the races.

Bishop's House
2222 E. Harris St.
Savannah, Ga.

August 23, 1916

Very Rev. Ignatius Lissner,
Provincial African Mission Fathers,
Savannah, Ga.

Very Rev. Dear Father Provincial:-

Your project of founding a Community of colored women for the purpose of the Christian education of the children of that race is a most excellent one, and, in view of the possibility of legislative interference with the work of white Sisters teaching them, in all probability a necessary one.

That there are many difficulties in the way of establishing this Community you are doubtless well aware, but if it be God's work it must meet opposition. To the thoughtless man it must seem strange that our Divine Lord, Who came to bring the blessings of liberty and peace to men and to show them the forgotten way to eternal happiness, foretold that the men, whom He would send to carry on and continue to the end of time this great work, would be hated by all men for His Name's sake, and that the day would come when men would deem it a service to God to put them to death....

We are experiencing to-day in Georgia the fulfillment of a part of this prophecy. A bitter campaign of misrepresentation and slander is being waged against the Catholic Church and its ministers....

Here in the South, as it seems to me, we have at our doors a mission field for mission activity.

Christ died for all — white and colored; and Christ's words are for the colored child as well: Let the little children come to Me. You are trying to bring the colored children to Christ that they may know, love and serve Him.

Be of good heart and do not be afraid. God will bless your efforts.

I give my full approbation to your most excellent plan, and bless it with all sincerity.

(Signed) +Benj. J. Keiley
Bishop of Savannah.

Archives of the Franciscan Handmaids of Mary, New York, with permission.

43. Chronicle of the Franciscan Handmaids of Mary, 1941

Reverend Father Lissner, a member of the Society of the African Missions came to America in 1897. He was a strong believer in colored priests and sisters who would work among their own race. He wished to establish a colored community who would educate the colored children, visit the sick, shelter the homeless and perform other works of charity.

His great problem was where to find someone interested enough to take this great responsibility. He tried many communities but was refused. Finally, he asked a priest, a friend of his, who referred him to a young lady (Barbara Williams), who at that time was in charge of the office for the Sisters of Notre Dame.[1] He immediately called her by phone, made an appointment. After an interview which lasted the whole afternoon, she very willingly accepted the responsibility.

Two years later the little community was established on East Gordon Street in a little frame house, under the title of the "Handmaids of the Most Pure Heart of Mary."

Archives of the Franciscan Handmaids of Mary, New York, with permission.

44. Decision to Form a Fraternal Order for Black Catholics, 1909

For much of the twentieth century, black Catholics were not welcomed in most Catholic fraternal organizations. Father Conrad Rebesher, a Josephite priest, pastor of a black parish in Mobile, saw the need for the Church to reach out to black Catholic laymen and make them active members of the Church. He organized the Knights of Peter Claver in 1909 with three other Josephite priests. In 1922, black women were formed into the Ladies of Peter Claver. Patterned after the Knights of Columbus, the Knights and Ladies of Peter Claver became in time one of the most important lay organizations among African American Catholics. In the following letter, Father Rebesher discussed his project for the new organization.

[The following line was written at the top of the letter.]

Dear Father, please read every line of this letter. Upon this letter depends a great deal. C.F.R.

Church Of The Most Pure Ht. Of Mary
Cor., Davis Ave., and Sengstak St.
Mobile, Alabama
Rev. C. F. Rebesher

September 16th, 1909

---

1. Elizabeth Barbara Williams was working at Trinity College, which belonged to the Sisters of Notre Dame de Namur in Washington, D.C.

Very Rev. Justin MacCarthy,
Baltimore, Md.

My dear Father MacCarthy:

When you were here in your last visitation, I mentioned to you, that it was my intention to organize a national association for the Colored men, along the same lines as the Knights of Columbus. The necessity and great need of such an organization, was clear to my mind, but I feared to undertake such a big task on my own initiative. Father Kelly, Van Baast, and myself had several meetings bearing on this matter, but did not arrive at any satisfactory conclusion. Naturaly [*sic*] enough we all hesitated, and well we might, because it is adding a great responsibility to those which are already ours. Nevertheless, the great negligence, and little interest of men in Church matters, and the constant falling away from the Faith, because of joining forbidden secret organizations, preyed on my mind heavily, and rest in this matter would not come to me; so after mature deliberation I decided to attempt organizing the men into a society called the "Knights of Peter Claver." A meeting was announced two weeks ahead of time, and yesterday the 15th, 32 meet at my house, many more being kept away by the rain. This was certainly an encouraging sign, and to see the interest these men took in the matter gave me great confidence of success. In the main we shall follow the Constitutions of the "Knights of Columbus," and the Ritual of Initiation for the first two degrees I have written up myself....

I remain yours obediently in Him,

Conrad

Souvenir Booklet, Knights of Peter Claver, 75th Jubilee Convention, New Orleans,
August 3–9, 1984, 18, with permission.

45. The Colored Knights in Convention, 1916

Gilbert Faustina, an African American from Mobile, was one of the founding members of the Knights of Peter Claver. The following presents part of his talk at a national convention in Mobile, 1916.

During August of the summer past the Knights of Peter Claver held their National Convention at Mobile, Ala. Mr. Gilbert Faustina, Supreme Knight, outlined a plan by which the members of the organization might increase their effectiveness in carrying on the good work for which the order was established. Part of his speech follows:

"From the showing we have made in the last twelve months, you can easily see that we are still a progressive organization, taking care of all our claims, and a snug amount to our credit in different banks.

"It may look small to some of us, the work our Order is doing for our people and Church over this South land, but you can believe me, Brother Knights, it will count in the future if every knight stands to his post. Dear Brothers, our people are in a very sad condition. You can easily see from the daily papers what I am saying is true. Our Mother Church is doing her part in various ways, and I might say there are many things we can do as an organization to better conditions for our people. Remember, our Patron, Saint Peter Claver, on the shores of Carthagena; glorious, indeed, the history of Peter Claver.

"There are too many of our people throwing up their hands and saying no use. That is the wrong way for them to speak and act and we, as Knights of Peter Claver, should resent the very thought of such ideas. Whatever you do, don't try to get away from your people; that one thing has done us more harm than any other. Get on the right road, roll up your sleeves and work for better conditions. They will come and come [in] fact if we only make the right kind of sacrifices and persevere to the end.

"Some will say, what can I do to better conditions? I will tell you in a few words right now what to do to better conditions.

"First be true Catholics and your neighbors will follow.

"Second, stand for your people, and your people will stand for better conditions.

"Third, build a Christian home, and the harvest will be great.

"And, above all, be true and tried Knights of Peter Claver, and let discipline be your first thought constantly. That will encourage others and I am positive that will make conditions far better than they are now all over the country.

"I consider this organization to be one of the Colored Catholics' opportunities to be of some use to their Church, and the Church to save the Colored man. Let us all try and make good of this opportunity at our door; we can if we will. The first thing for us to do is to stick together and work hard; and I might say there is scarcely a sane average moderately healthy man that could not end life comfortable and prosperous, if he would seize the two possibilities always with us — hard work and economy.

The Colored Harvest 8, no. 1 (January 1916): 11, with permission.

46. Father Peter Janser, S.V.D., Informs the American Bishops of the Establishment of a Seminary to Teach Black Students for the Priesthood, 1921

By the first decade of the twentieth century the Josephites made the decision to no longer encourage black students for the priesthood. This was partly the result of the American bishops' unwillingness to welcome African American priests to work in their dioceses. The Society of the Divine Word, a missionary society founded by German priests in 1875, began working among African Americans in Mississippi in 1905. The question of ordaining young black men to the priesthood was critical to any effort to evangelize the black community. Despite the not-so-subtle opposition to an African American priesthood, the Divine Word Missionaries began an all-black seminary first in Greenville, Mississippi, and then in Bay St. Louis on the Gulf. The Divine Word Missionaries obtained the support and the approbation of the Holy See, which traditionally had always supported a native clergy as part of its missionary activities. As a result, in November 1921, the provincial Father Peter Janser wrote a letter to all the bishops in the United States informing them that the seminary college would be moved from Greenville to Bay St. Louis the following year.

I feel that you will be interested in an account of the work for the education of colored boys to the Catholic priesthood, which the Society of the Divine Word undertook about a year ago.

For the past sixteen years our Fathers have been successfully laboring among the colored people of our country. But since our work was generally among the Protestants, unusual difficulties stood in the way. On account of the many restrictions imposed upon the missionaries by the existing social conditions, our activity was almost entirely limited to the school room with the natural result that progress has been very slow. Thus the conviction grew upon us that the conversion of the colored RACE could not be looked for, unless there would be a COLORED CLERGY, as non-Catholic denominations had provided them ever since the Civil War.

We realized the difficulties of having a colored SECULAR clergy; but after many conferences with competent men, including several members of our American hierarchy, we could find no valid or serious objection to a colored RELIGIOUS priesthood. It is to the Right Rev. John E. Gunn, Bishop of Natchez, that most credit is due for carrying out this plan. He had always been a zealous shepherd of his colored children, and so very generously consented to have the beginning made in his diocese, at Greenville, Washington Co., Miss.

While the "Sacred Heart College" found a temporary home at Greenville, a more suitable property has been acquired at Bay Saint Louis, Miss., where the institution will be permanently established to be known then as ST. AUGUSTINE'S MISSION HOUSE.

As you will note above, the candidates will be trained for the religious life of Priests and Brothers. At the suggestion of the Roman authorities the plan of an AUTONOMOUS province has been decided upon. Hence, while all are candidates of the Society of the Divine Word, they will receive their education in separate institutions. Remaining under the same Superior General, and, for many years to come, under white local and provincial superiors, they will ultimately form a province of their own. It is our ambition to train them according to the purpose of our Society, for missionary work among their own people, both here in the United States and eventually also in foreign countries.

We are pleased to tell your Lordship that twenty-eight candidates for the colored priesthood are studying today at Sacred Heart College, Greenville, Miss. As a rule, only the best boys of Catholic parents are accepted. It has been very gratifying that the priests and sisters laboring among the colored people have enthusiastically welcomed our foundation, and we are particularly grateful for the promise of their faithful cooperation....

You are, no doubt, aware, my dear Bishop, that we have assumed a very difficult task. It is well known that the work of educating colored boys for a religious priesthood does not make the strong appeal to many people that it should make. More than ordinary patience and prudence will be required, and only God's special blessing can make this work a success. Since we believe it to be His work, we trust in Him, the more so, since we have no other end in view than to win souls for Christ, to prepare for the ultimate conversion of the whole colored race, and to do this by the most efficient means. You have often heard the missionary axiom, universally recognized as such, that no people has ever been converted except by men of their own blood.

The Holy Father himself has but recently given strong expression to this truth, and he sure did not wish to exclude the Negroes of the United States. Brazil has shown the way. A colored Catholic Archbishop is admired there for his scholarship and sanctity; our own Fathers are working under his jurisdiction. Besides, over 200 Negro priests are giving an excellent account of themselves.

The race problem has become a troublesome one and may lead to a crisis. While we do not consider it within the scope of our activity to seek directly for a solution of the social, economic, or even political aspect of that problem, we think the best solution would be to make the NEGRO CATHOLIC. It is his birthright as much as ours, of which he has been too long deprived.

In submitting this statement to your Lordship, it is not only to obviate misunderstandings, but to ask for advice and guidance. Though principally an organization for foreign mission work, we are nevertheless desirous of being helpful at home and do some missionary work, where we can lighten the burden of some of our bishops. We hope to do our work quietly, without hurting the susceptibilities of opponents; but you will agree with us that

God's holy will and the wish of the Holy Father should not be frustrated by prejudice and lack of charity.

In conclusion, may I humbly ask for your Episcopal blessing and the alms of prayer for our Community, our whole mission work, and especially for the young seminary? With the assurance of profoundest respect, I beg to remain, Your Lordship's most obedient servant....

William Bonner, *Chronologium,* Society of Divine Word Archives, Techny, Illinois, as cited in Ernest Brandewie, *In the Light of the Word: Divine Word Missionaries of North America* (Maryknoll, N.Y.: Orbis Books, 2000), 220–21, with permission.

47. Pope Pius XI Writes to the Superior General of the Society of the Divine Word to Give Support for the Education of African American Men to the Priesthood, 1923

Although the Catholic clergy in the United States gave little support to the idea of a black Catholic priesthood, the Holy See welcomed the notion of educating a black Catholic priesthood. Concerned about the lack of conversion to the Catholic Church among African Americans, the popes recalled on numerous occasions that the conversion of a people depended upon the growth of a clergy from its midst. In this letter Pius XI gives enthusiastic support to the Divine Word Missioners in taking up the charge of educating black Catholic priests. This letter of Pius XI is only one of many examples during this period when Rome gave support to the African American Catholic community.

Pius XI
to His Son, William Gier, Superior General
of the Society of the Divine Word

Beloved Son!
Greeting and Apostolic Blessing

It is to Us a source of deep joy to learn that the college for the education of Negroes which you had established temporarily at Greenville, in the Diocese of Natchez, will shortly be transferred to Bay St. Louis, in the same diocese, and converted into a mission house for training of Negro boys according to the Rule of your Order....In your new undertaking you are following the very principle which, in so far as circumstances allowed, has always guided the Catholic Church. To this mother has arisen, especially in recent times, a numerous progeny among the black races — a host of children who have frequently displayed virtues so splendid that they sealed their faith with their blood as in the most glorious epochs of Christian history. The Negroes occupy enormous areas of the earth, and it is undoubted that these races, which the Church takes so loving and maternal an interest in gladdening with the knowledge of her joyful message, will in the course of time be trained in all branches of human civilization, and will thus arise from their present lowly stage of culture, and attain a high level in their mode of life and moral training. If, therefore, we wish to accomplish some useful and solid work in this field, it is indispensable that priests of the same race shall make it their life-task to lead these peoples to the Christian faith.... You, beloved son, regard it as a very practical step to admit into the Society of the Divine Word Negroes who give evidence of a vocation for the regular life. These candidates are later to be admitted to the priesthood and eventually work as apostles among the members of their race. You have chosen this path because you are firmly convinced that the Negroes can thus be brought much more easily and rapidly into the Church, and also because, in the spirit of true filial obedience, you wish to follow the guidance of Our immediate Predecessor. In his Apostolic Brief of November 30, 1919, the latter gives a list of practical suggestions and precepts to which no reasonable man can take exception. For does it not indeed follow, as Our Predecessor points out, from the very nature of the Church as a Divine institution that every tribe or people should have priests who are one with it in race and character, in habit of thought and temperament? ... Moreover, as experience has shown, the young Negro is not poorly gifted, mentally, so that he cannot assimilate higher education and the theological sciences....

You have, therefore, undertaken a most laudable work, beloved son, in which to engage your zeal for the faith and for souls. In order that your success may be all the more gratifying you will pray with Us to Our Divine Savior that the Negro youth may hear and obey His divine injunction: "Go ye also into my vineyard." The Negroes of the United States greatly exceed ten million souls, for whom a capable mission and secular clergy of their own race must be created as soon as possible.

May the Blessed Virgin, Queen of Apostles, take under her protection this undertaking in which We wish you, beloved son, and your whole Society success....

May the Holy Doctor St. Augustine, under whose protection you have appropriately placed the seminary, also implore for the Negro race that fullness of the light of Christian knowledge which, as history shows, once suffused the fields of Africa!

Finally, beloved son, in so far as We are concerned, rest assured that We are most anxious to do everything to promote this salutary undertaking....

PIUS XI POPE

ROME, ST. PETER'S, April 5, 1923,
In the second year of Our Pontificate.

St. Augustine Seminary Archives, Bay St. Louis, Mississippi, copy translated from original, with permission.

Part 7

MID-CENTURY: WINDS OF CHANGE

48. Claude McKay, Poet of the Harlem Renaissance, Convert, 1946–47

The Harlem Renaissance was a period following the First World War when Harlem became a center for African American writers, poets, playwrights, painters, musicians, and artists of all varieties. The Jamaican poet Claude McKay was one of the leading figures in this cultural movement. McKay was born in Jamaica in 1890 and came to the United States in 1912. He lived for a while in Russia (1922–23), where he became a member of the Communist Party and then became disillusioned. He spent several years in southern France, Spain, and Morocco before returning to the United States in 1934. To the consternation of his friends, he converted to Catholicism in 1944. He died in 1948. His poetry after his conversion is not as well known as the poems of an earlier period. Three examples from his Catholic period follow. The third example was the result of a short stay at St. Meinrad Archabbey, a Benedictine monastery in Indiana, in the summer after his conversion.

THE WORD

The Word was God and God He was the Word!
How beautiful, majestic and sublime,
The Word of Man becomes the Sovereign Lord
Of Earth and Sea and Heaven for all time.
Lord of my word, inventor of all words,
Supreme Creator of the Word, Oh God
Who made our words to be as free as birds,
To sing and wing and ring when angels nod!

Thy Word, Thy lovely Music that should lift
Men up to know the grandly magnified,
Oh Lord, Thy wonderful and precious gift
We have betrayed, ignobly crucified.

Oh, spread Thy words like green fields, watered, fresh,
The Word is God and the Word is made flesh!

Catholic Worker 14, no. 5 (July–August 1947): 2.

TRUTH

Lord, shall I find it in Thy Holy Church,
Or must I give it up as something dead,
Forever lost, no matter where I search.
Like dinosaurs within their ancient bed?
I found it not in years of Unbelief
In science stirring life like budding trees,
In Revolution like a dazzling thief
Oh, shall I find it on my bended knees?

Oh, what is Truth, so Pilate asked Thee, Lord.
Two thousand years when Thou wert manifest,
As the Eternal and Incarnate Word.
Chosen of God and by Him singly blest;
In this vast world of lies and hate and greed,
Upon my knees, Oh Lord, for Truth I plead.

Catholic Worker 12 (January 1946): 3.

SAINT MEINRAD

How excellently there among the hills
Saint Meinrad sets her lovely self, and stands,
A wonder to the land on which she spills
The richness flowing from her active hands.
From far and near her children seek this place,
And humbly sit them at their elders' feet,
To hear the story of Christ's wondrous grace,
And learn God's wisdom in this blest retreat.

Oh, there are lovely regions on the earth,
God has provided for the good of man,
To turn from mundane ways and seek new birth
To live again as surely as man can!
Such is Saint Meinrad chosen by the Lord,
To propagate His everlasting Word.

Personal Records and Papers, Placidus Kempf, Box 3, Correspondence 1924–69, St. Meinrad Archabbey Archives, published in the student publication *The Crusade Beacon* (April 1946): 3.

Claude McKay's conversion to Catholicism was especially important for Catholics in the 1940s. McKay was both an ex-Communist and a militant black man who had an international reputation. His former friends and associates, most of them Socialists and left-wing activists, found it difficult to believe in the sincerity of his conversion. The following is an article in a popular Catholic periodical from New York. It is McKay's explanation of why he became a Catholic.

On Becoming a Roman Catholic

When the director of the Sheil School of Social Studies, George Drury, who made the arrangements for my baptism, asked if I desired any publicity, I said no. I said that if I were publishing an article or a poem or a book, then I should state the fact, since I was always known as a pagan writer. Otherwise, it was like letting the world in on a quiet ceremony between a man and his God. This would have something of the odor of an inter-racial marriage touted by the newspapers to make an American sensation. Marriage is a sacrament, difficult enough even between persons of a similar group. Why, then, make a mixed marriage more of a problem by invidious publicity, which focuses the eyes of the world on the couple! Similarly, in my opinion, a man's religion is not a sensation to titillate the appetite of the public. It is a sacred thing to keep and to hold fast between him and his God.

When His Excellency, Bishop Bernard J. Sheil of the Archdiocese of Chicago, was informed by my friend Mary Jerdo (formerly of Harlem Friendship House) that I was deeply interested in the Roman Catholic faith and wanted to become a Catholic, the Bishop replied that that with me was an intellectual matter. An intellectual matter it has been ever since I began thinking seriously about the Catholic Faith in 1938 until I was baptized on October 11, 1944 the Feast Day of the Maternity of the Blessed Virgin.

I was always religious-minded as some of my pagan poems attest. But I never had any faith in revealed religion! My parents sent me to live with my eldest brother and start my preliminary education, when I was six years old. My brother was the school teacher and lay reader for an Anglican church. He also was an agnostic. He lived in a more refined region of the island, near the sea, and quite different from the wild, rolling hills, among which I first saw the light. My sister-in-law put shoes on my feet, an Eton collar around my neck and sent me to school. By the time I was ten, my brother was pushing free-thinking books my way. I devoured Huxley and Lecky, Haeckel and Gibbon and others. My sister-in-law was very religious. When she saw me reading Haeckel's *The Riddle of the Universe*, she said it was a bad book, and tried to stop me. My brother said: "Let the boy read anything he likes."

...I went to Tuskegee, which I considered a wonderful school of all-Negro students and teachers. But after a few months I left it for the Kansas State College, where I studied for over two years. Then I left for New York. I went to work at any job a young Negro could find. But I still kept up the writing of poems.

The way had already been prepared, when I arrived in the United States, to take me to Max Eastman and the Socialists. He appointed me to be his assistant on the *Liberator.* I had imbibed Fabian Socialism with my mother's milk, so to speak....

...I visited Russia soon after the Revolution. It was a shock to find there a government and a society basically anti-human nature. It rested upon the theory that the working-class could not better itself and take power, except by civil war with wholesale slaughtering of other workers and the middle and upper classes. So I left them alone and moved on to sample the rest of Europe. I swung around from place to place in the circle of disillusioned liberals and radicals, I forgot about social revolution. Instead I wrote risqué stories and novels. At that time that was the fashion in writing.

Years before in London, Bernard Shaw had impressed me with a long talk about the beauty of medieval cathedrals and how to look at them. Now on the continent of Europe, in France and in Spain, I had leisure for visiting and contemplation in the cathedrals. I lifted my head up at the great Gothic arches and was overwhelmed by their beauty. It was in Europe that I saw the vision of the grandeur and glory of the Roman Catholic religion.

I loved the people of Catholic Spain. It was the first time I ever fell in love with any people, colored or white, as a whole. But Spaniards of all classes have such a fundamental understanding of the dignity of the individual and the oneness of all Humanity. I discovered in Spain that Catholicism had made of the Spanish people the most noble and honest and humane of any in the world, while Protestantism had made of the Anglo-Saxons and their American cousins, the vilest, hoggish and most predatory and hypocritical people in the world As a pagan I had always accepted without thinking clearly about it, that Catholic countries were the most backward and unprogressive in the world. But Spain taught me that progress was not with the "progressives."

I had often said that if ever I became a Christian, I would choose the Roman Catholic Faith, by which I could submit to authority. But I never thought that it would ever happen. I might have chosen to become a Roman Catholic in Spain. But Spaniards, priests and laity, are not proselytizers. They have the spirit of God. So, when after 12 years in Europe and North Africa, I returned to the United States, I was still an agnostic....

Ellen Tarry, writer of children's books, and I met in 1938. She is a Roman Catholic, the only Catholic intellectual among Harlem's hectic mélange of pagans and Protestants. I was smarting under the Communist's attack on my recent book, *A Long Way From Home*. Tarry talked to me about Friendship House in Harlem....

Ellen Tarry said: "Claude, why don't you become a Catholic? It is the only religion for a man like you who has traveled all over and seen everything." I said: "But, Tarry, I am an unbeliever, an agnostic." She replied: "It is easier for an intellectual not to believe than to believe." These words set me thinking hard, for I do not like taking things easy. I had always believed with the pagan apologists that Christianity had destroyed the glory of pagan life. To be sure about it I started reading some books about the Roman Empire in its decadence.... Then I saw clearly that pagan society was more corrupt than the society that developed under Christianity....

I was flooded by the True Light. I discovered a little of that mystical world of the spirit that eludes the dictators, the agnostics, the pure materialists. I saw too, the Roman Catholic Church in a light different, indeed, from the manner in which I had previously visioned it...I became very ill and hid myself away from my friends. Ellen Tarry discovered where I was, and brought along some girls from Friendship House to nurse me. Among them I met Mary Jerdo. She was the intellectual type, and we discovered much in common. My illness extended through many months. In the summer of 1943 Mary sent me up to her little cottage in a solitary spot of Connecticut.

In those days pecuniary help came from a few left wing liberals, Freda Kirchway, Max Eastman and friends of the *New Leader*. My week-end visitors were former Stalinists, disillusioned Trotskyites, and Anarchists! I thought that if I were to die, it would be these people, whose ideas and views I had altogether repudiated, who would take charge of my body. That thought made me more than ever eager to become a Catholic. In the spring of 1944 Mary Jerdo, through Bishop Sheil, invited me out to Chicago. That fall I was baptized by the Paulist, Father Roach of Old St. Mary's.

Claude McKay, "On Becoming a Roman Catholic," *The Epistle: A Quarterly Bulletin* 11, no. 2 (Spring 1945): 43–45, with permission.

49. *The Third Door: The Autobiography of an American Negro Woman,* by Ellen Tarry, 1955

Ellen Tarry was one of the African American writers who were part of the Harlem Renaissance. Originally from Birmingham, Alabama, she became a Catholic as a young girl when she was a student at Rock Castle Academy in Virginia, a school for girls run by the Sisters of the Blessed Sacrament.

She went to Harlem, where she became part of the flood tide of African American culture in the 1920s and 1930s. It was here that she met Claude McKay and was instrumental in his conversion to Catholicism. The following is a section from her autobiography.

A few Sundays after...Father Mulvoy spoke to me after the last Mass. "Ellen," he said, "there's a white woman across the street at Number 48 who came down from Canada to help me with the social work of the parish. She escaped from Russia during the Revolution and knows all about the Communists. I'm counting on you to help her. Go over there and meet her."

"She should meet Claude [McKay] instead of me," I thought as I crossed 138th Street to Number 48 and rang the bell beneath the name of Catherine de Hueck.[1] After climbing three flights of steps I found myself in a one-room apartment dominated by a handsome blonde woman of large stature. I saw many stacks of books.

"I'm Catherine de Hueck," the woman smiled after I explained that Father Mulvoy had sent me. "You are wondering about the books, aren't you?"

"Why so many of them?" I asked. "And what are you going to do with them?"

"My friends sent them from the Friendship House Library," she said.

"Where *is* Friendship House?"

"Why, you poor child," she said. "*This* is Friendship House. You must come around Monday night when the Newmanites meet here...."

I went to the Monday night meeting. It would be truer to say the meeting met me as I climbed the steps. Boys and girls were standing on the stairway, leaning against the banisters, sitting wherever they could....I sat on the floor next to an attractive Creole-looking girl....Across the room was one brown-skinned boy. Though the others were talking about my people I could tell that few of them had known or associated with Negroes.

I could catch phrases like "the Fatherhood of God, and the Brotherhood of man" or "the Negro and the Mystical Body" which indicated much more depth than I had attributed to these youngsters. Then the Baroness talked about "Christ in the Negro" and along with all the others in the room I came under the spell of Catherine de Hueck. I was convinced that Friendship House needed me and many other Negroes if it was to be the Catholic Center the Baroness had said was needed to combat the forces of Godless

---

1. The Baroness Catherine de Hueck was born in Russia in 1896. She played an important role in the apostolate to African Americans by the establishment of Friendship Houses in many large cities. She died in Canada in 1985. [Ed.]

Communism in Harlem. But I would have to get more Negroes to help me and we would have to explain to these well-intentioned white boys and girls that, instead of working for the Negro, they would have to work *with* us.

Ellen Tarry, *The Third Door: The Autobiography of an American Negro Woman* (New York: David McKay Company, Inc., 1955), 142–44, with permission.

Part 8

CIVIL RIGHTS AND AFRICAN AMERICAN CATHOLICS

Black Catholics were not on the front line of the civil rights movement in the beginning. There were individuals like A. P. Tureaud, a leading black Catholic attorney in New Orleans, who joined Thurgood Marshall and other civil rights lawyers who fought the battle for racial justice in the courts. Black Catholics were often participants in demonstrations on the local level, but black Catholic priests led the Church into a prophetic role on the American scene in the mid-1960s. Early on, black Catholic theologians began to discuss the question of black theology in the context of Catholic theology. Their contribution was a turning point in the religious development of Catholics in the racial conflict of the times.

50. A Statement of the Black Catholic Clergy Caucus, 1968

This statement was drawn up by black Catholic priests in Detroit at the Sheraton-Cadillac Hotel. Although the Catholic Clergy Conference on the Interracial Apostolate was holding its annual meeting, the black priests present had decided to meet in caucus to discuss the racial crisis that had gripped the nation in the wake of the assassination of Martin Luther King Jr. at the beginning of the month. The assembled priests were faced with the question of what they should do as leaders and as priests. This statement reflected their anguish and their anger. This was the first time that black priests had ever come together in a body in the history of the Church in the United States.

The Catholic Church in the United States, primarily a white racist institution, has addressed itself primarily to white society and is definitely a part of that society. On the contrary, we feel that her primary, though not exclusive work, should be in the area of institutional, attitudinal and societal change. Within the ghetto, the role of the Church is no longer that of spokesman and leader. Apart from a more direct spiritual role, the Church's part must now be that of supporter and learner. This is a role that white priests in the black community have not been accustomed to playing and are not psychologically prepared to play.

The Catholic Church apparently is not cognizant of changing attitudes in the black community and is not making the necessary, realistic adjustments. The present attitude of the black community demands that black people control their own affairs and make decisions for themselves. This does not mean, however, that black leadership is to be exercised only in the black community, but must function throughout the entire gamut of ecclesial society.

It is imperative that the Church recognize this change. White persons working in the black community must be educated to these changing attitudes, and must be prepared to accept and function in conjunction with the prevailing attitudes of the black community.

One of these changes must be a re-evaluation of present attitudes towards black militancy. The violence occurring in the black communities has been *categorically* condemned and has called forth a wide variety of response, from "shoot to kill" to the recommendation of the Kerner Report. Such violence has even been specified as "Negro violence," as though there were a substantial or significant difference between violence in the black community and that which has occurred consistently throughout the history of the United States and of the world. Black people are fully aware that violence has been consciously and purposely used by America from its fight for independence to its maintenance of white supremacy. Since the black man is encouraged to fight abroad for white America's freedom and liberty, we are now asking why it is not moral for him to fight for his liberty at home. We go on record as recognizing:

1. the reality of militant protest;

2. that non-violence in the sense of black non-violence hoping for concessions after white brutality is dead;

3. that the same principles on which we justify legitimate self-defense and just warfare must be applied to violence when it represents black response to white violence;

4. the appropriateness of responsible, positive militancy against racism is the only Christian attitude against this or any other social evil.

Because of its past complicity with and active support of prevailing attitudes and institutions of America, the Church is now in an extremely weak position in the black community. In fact, the Catholic Church is rapidly dying in the black community. In many areas, there is a serious defection especially on the part of black Catholic youth. The black community no longer looks to the Catholic Church with hope. And unless the Church, by an immediate, effective and total reversing of its present practices, rejects and denounces all forms of racism within its ranks and institutions and in the society of which she is a part, she will become unacceptable in the black community.

We, **The Black Catholic Clergy Caucus**, strongly and deeply believe that there are few choices left to the Catholic Church, and unless it is to remain an enclave speaking to itself, it must begin to consult the black members of the Church, clerical, religious and lay. It must also begin to utilize the personnel resources of black Catholics in leadership and advisory positions in the whole Church and allow them to direct, for the most part, the mission of the Church in the black community. It is especially important that the financial resources channeled into the work of the Church in the black community be allocated and administered by black Catholic leadership. To this end, in charity, we demand:

1. That there be black priests in decision-making positions on the diocesan level, and above all in the black community.

2. That a more effective utilization of black priests be made. That the situation where the majority of black priests are in institutions be changed; that black priests be given a choice of assignment on the basis of inclination and talent.

3. That where no black priests belong to the diocese, efforts be made to get them in or at least consultation with black priests or black-thinking white priests be made.

4. That special efforts be made to recruit black men for the priesthood. Black priests themselves are better qualified for this recruitment at a time when the Catholic Church is almost irrelevant to the young black men.

5. That dioceses provide centers of training for white priests intending to survive in black communities.

6. That within the framework of the United States Catholic Conference, a black-directed department be set up to deal with the Church's role in the struggle of black people for freedom.

7. That in all of these areas black religious be utilized as much as possible.

8. That black men, married as well as single, be ordained permanent deacons to aid in this work of the Church.

9. That each diocese allocate a substantial fund to be used in establishing and supporting permanent programs for black leadership training.

> "A Statement of the Black Catholic Clergy Caucus," in *Black Theology: A Documentary History,* Volume 1: 1966–1979, 2nd ed. revised, ed. James H. Cone and Gayraud S. Wilmore (Maryknoll, N.Y.: Orbis Books, 1993), 230–32; originally in *Freeing the Spirit* 1, no. 3 (1972), with permission.

51. The Survival of Soul: National Black Sisters' Conference Position Paper, 1969

Just as the black priests formed themselves into a national body in response to the civil rights movement and the subsequent racial unrest in the nation, black Catholic Sisters formed themselves into a Black Sisters' Conference at the University of Dayton in Dayton, Ohio, in August 1969. The sisters drew up a position paper in which they specified their goals as black Catholic religious women in this period of racial crisis.

We, the members of the National Black Sisters' Conference, pledge ourselves to work unceasingly for the liberation of black people. We black religious women see ourselves as gifted with the choicest of God's blessings. The gift of our womanhood, that channel through which the Son of God Himself chose to come into the human race, endows us with those qualities and prerogatives which are designed for the deliverance of humanity. The gift of our blackness gives us our mandate for the deliverance of a special people, our own black folk. And the gift of our religious vocation makes accessible to us that union with Christ which guides us to the task, strengthens our determination, and sustains our efforts to free ourselves and our black brethren from the intolerable burden forced upon us as the victims of white racism.

The reality in American society today makes it inescapably clear to us that our attempt to free black people must begin with a forthright denunciation of the problem recognizable as white racism. Expressions of individual and institutional racism found in our society and within our Church are declared by us to be categorically evil and inimical to the freedom of all men everywhere, and particularly destructive of black people in America. We are cognizant of our responsibility to witness to the dignity of all persons as creatures of God, and are acutely aware of the fact that failure to denounce white racism, in fact, perpetuates this evil. Moreover, our failure to speak out against this evil exposes us to the risk of miscarrying and betraying that sacred trust which God our Father has seen fit to place in our hands.

Because our primary goal is the liberation of black people, our first concern is to assess the condition in which we black folk find ourselves, as a result of the problem of white racism. We note that the effect of this evil upon us is such that we are now in a position of relative powerlessness, suffering overwhelming poverty, and victimized by a crippling distorted self-image. Our powerlessness is reflected in every social institution of American society, including the Church; our impoverishment affects every area of our lives; our distorted self-image permeates almost all of our relationships. We black sisters cannot and will not tolerate any longer this total destruction of a great people.

Despite the aforementioned liabilities, black folk have retained and employed resourcefully those assets which are ours by the grace of God. We black sisters are fully aware of that great *wealth of person* which is the rich heritage of black people in America. We appreciate most deeply that total black experience, that indefinable yet identifiable "soul" which is our proud possession. We draw strength and courage from that patient, unflagging *endurance* which has characterized us as a victimized people. And we shout "Glory! Halleluia!" with that *hope* which rests in our hearts as a rich largesse from God, our Father, through His Son, Jesus Christ.

These personal assets in which we glory, and for which we praise and thank God, are not the sum total of our possessions as a people. Over and above these is that greatest of all gifts, that *communal concern* of black folk for their own people....

Within this context, we believe it is necessary to express ourselves as black religious women, and through the following objectives and these initially proposed programs, to chart our course of action to the end that all may be free, and in that freedom to become one in God.

1. *Objective:* To importune our society, especially our Church and religious congregations to respond with Christian enthusiasm to the need for eradicating the powerlessness, the poverty, and the distorted self-image of victimized black people by responsibly encouraging white people to address themselves to the roots of racism in their own social, professional and spiritual milieu....

2. *Objective:* To help promote a positive self-image among ourselves, in our black folk, especially in our black youth, through knowledge of and appreciation for the beauty of our rich historical and cultural heritage....

3. *Objective:* To stimulate community action aimed at the achievement of social, political, and economic black power and to participate in

programs that exist already in the civic communities of which we are members....

4. *Objective and Proposed Action:* To initiate, organize and/or participate in self-help programs through which we can educate ourselves and our black people, thereby encouraging the utilization of those resources which are useful to black people....

5. *Objective:* To employ the energies of the National Black Sisters' Conference for the development of the personal resources of individual sisters for the deepening of our spirituality and for the promotion of unity and solidarity among black religious women....

6. *Objective:* To develop and utilize fully the potential represented by the National Black Sisters' Conference through effective participation in the Central Office for Black Catholicism, and through initiation and endorsement of all activities and programs which can support and enhance the growth of black religious leadership within the Church and in our religious communities....

National Black Sisters' Conference, *Black Survival: Past, Present, Future* (National Black Sisters' Conference, August 6–16, 1969), 155–59, with permission.

52. Lawrence Lucas, A Black Priest Faces the Reality of Racism in the Catholic Church, 1970

Father Lucas, articulate, witty, angry, and well-informed, became the spokesperson for many black priests in the civil rights struggle. A priest of the Archdiocese of New York, he wrote one of the most stirring critiques of the racial attitudes of American Catholics in a book entitled Black Priest/White Church. *Father Lucas was one of the founding members of the National Black Catholic Clergy Caucus. At times he worked alone and was not fully appreciated. His writings captured the feelings of anger and frustration of a generation of black Catholics.*

The best example I can give of how the Church makes black people white, or want to be, is myself. I say this without shame. Practically all black people in this country, regardless of what institution they belong to, have gone or will go through this. Some will make it through sooner, others later. Some won't make it out of the white man's bag. To the extent that I am out is due in no small measure to my encounter with Malcolm X. This relationship began a whole new way of looking at myself and others and things and events. It is impossible for me to forget that I am the product of the Church's system that transforms black people into black-faced white people....

Malcolm and I ran into each other on 126th Street and Seventh Avenue in Harlem one morning. I was dressed in the black-suit, black-tie and white-shirt uniform of seminarians. He stopped me to ask what I was about.

"I'm going to school."

"I surmise that," he retorted. "What are you doing there?"

"I'm studying."

"That's nice, what?"

"To be a Roman Catholic priest."

I'll never forget his expression. In those days most Negroes would have salaamed twice; here was an exceptional Negro whom white folks had accepted. Malcolm stood in his tracks, looked me straight in the eyes, and said, "Are you out of your God damned mind?" A few chats later I began to understand what he meant. Today I see the full, horrible truth.

The full, horrible truth is that the Church wrecks black minds. This is not unique to the Catholic Church, obviously Christianity in America has hardly been geared to the black man's interests. The most devastating effect of Catholicism on Negroes has been the loss of their minds as black people.

...I intend to be a black man and remain a priest in a white racist Church. I will caucus, organize, plan with black people and accept white support to make real a black Jesus Who will call together and form a black people through whom He will save the Church and America. Like others, I will continue to speak out — to retrieve the minds of Negro Catholics from the man's captivity, and to encourage white Catholics to start believing what they say they do and to start behaving the way they talk. When white Catholics start acting toward black people the way they teach black people to act toward them, the problem will be solved. If we black people fail, all — black and white — will go down together.

I have made this choice because I feel there is more to the Catholic Church than white racists. I still believe the Church is a divine *and* human, a free and responsive community of faith, hope and charity called into being, nourished, sustained and missioned by Father, Son and Spirit. I believe the community is to be achieved by sacrament, word, and ministry and that it is called to be the Sacrament of the saving unity and presence of Jesus Christ in the world today and until all is reconciled to the Father.

Lawrence Lucas, *Black Priest/White Church: Catholics and Racism* (New York: Random House, 1970), 11–13, 267, with permission.

53. Joseph Davis, The Beginning of the National Office for Black Catholics, 1970

The founding of the National Black Catholic Clergy Caucus in 1968 served as a catalyst for the formation of other black Catholic organizations, most notably the formation of the black sisters and later the black seminarians. Soon it became apparent that a type of umbrella association was needed to represent the black Catholic community as a whole. This resulted in the formation of NOBC. The first director was Joseph Davis, S.M., a Marianist brother at that time. In the following document, Brother Joseph Davis recounts his personal reflection on the first days of the first civil rights black Catholic organization.

The gathering of Black clergy took place in Detroit in April, 1968. Approximately fifty to seventy-five of the nation's one hundred and fifty Black priests were in attendance. In addition, Sr. Martin de Porres Grey, R.S.M., and I were present as observers. The majority of the meeting was devoted to an assessment of the situation of the Black community in general, the state of the Catholic Church in the Black community, utilization of Black clergy and the status of Black vocations. . . .

The National Black Sisters' Conference was organized in the summer of 1968 under the leadership of Sr. Martin de Porres Grey, an intelligent, articulate, highly skilled Black nun from Pittsburgh. By the summer of 1969 lay Black Catholics had organized, with the initial meeting taking place at the Catholic University in Washington, D.C. With that meeting, new Black Catholic organizations forged in the crucible of the Black nationalist period were causing the Catholic Church to confront the reality of its one million Black members, the racism in its structure, and to take a stance on race relations in the country.

Black and Catholic. For these new Black Catholic organizations, the temper of the times called for unequivocal identification with the needs, hurts, and aspirations of Black people, pride in identifying culturally with Black Americans and with Africa, and demonstration of a willingness to join the ranks of other Black organizations in the frontline struggle. . . .

Black clergy (including priests and brothers), religious sisters and laity each formed national organizations, and structured themselves into regional units. Numerous regional and diocesan conferences began to take place across the country, all raising the issue of the lack of significant Black participation in the church, the absence of Black Catholics in diocesan and national leadership positions, the presence of only one Black bishop among the three hundred and sixty members of the hierarchy, the lack of "fit" between Catholic liturgy and Black cultural traditions. One of the truly

Brother Joseph Davis, S.M. (1937–92). First director of the National Office for Black Catholics. Reprinted with permission of the Marianist Archives, St. Louis.

remarkable contributions of Black Catholics to the American Catholic Church in general was the fact that the three organizations quickly developed cooperative ties, mapped out a common agenda, and worked closely together in negotiating with the institution to meet their goal. An early model of cooperative ecclesiology was being shaped in the process, and it would come to fruition for a time in the structure of the board of directors of the National Office for Black Catholics (NOBC). The board was intentionally structured in such a way that the combined number of male clergy and religious, and female religious members was equal to that of the lay members. In other words, in voting strength, the lay members had the greater voice. The vision and purpose was to demonstrate in a practical way a new spirit of shared responsibility within the Church.

The response of the Church to the initial Black Clergy statement was one of shock. The rapid organizing of women religious and lay Catholics, both supporting the clergy statement, increased the unease of the hierarchy and clearly necessitated a response. Father Rollins Lambert, who had been elected president of the Black Catholic Clergy Caucus, met with then Bishop John Wright, chairman of the United States Catholic Conference Committee on Social Development and World Peace, in Pittsburgh to discuss the Clergy statement, the Black movement, and consider possible responses by the Church. The Black Clergy, Sisters and Lay Caucuses chose a core group of representatives to form a planning group to pursue the implications of the call for a Black vicariate. The National Conference of Catholic Bishops made an initial allocation of $16,000.00 which allowed the planning group to get seriously under way... over a period of twelve months a comprehensive plan for a national office for Black Catholics replaced the idea of a vicariate. The plan called for a budget of $500,000.00 to implement programs. The NCCB designated an ad-hoc committee to meet and negotiate with the Black Catholic planning group....

In its November, 1969 meeting, the National Conference of Catholic Bishops officially received the proposal, debated it, and approved an allocation of $150,000.00 — far short of what the proposal called for and what Black Catholics envisioned. Black Catholics learned of the NCCB action in one of the regularly scheduled NCCB press conferences, and on the spot made the decision not to accept "one penny of the racist money." Again the bishops were stung and stunned. Black Catholics felt some moments of exhilaration at boldly rejecting this tiny opening. Then the reality set in that if there was going to be a National Office for Black Catholics, Black Catholics would have to find a way to finance it themselves. In this period of self-determination and self-reliance there was a resolve to push ahead and work with whatever funds could be generated....

During all this time, what had been set out as an ideal vision of what NOBC really represented — a new spirit of collaboration among clergy, religious and laity — increasingly became its greatest point of tension. The National Office for Black Catholics had purposely avoided setting itself up as a membership organization. It claimed and made an effort to represent the entire Black Catholic community in the U.S. The three Caucuses were the membership organizations. It was up to them to develop their own constituencies.... The challenge was to maintain a corporate ownership, as opposed to seeing it as the laity's organization or the clergy's organization. This required some delicate maneuvering among the groups and with the board of directors where all three came together. It was a difficulty never adequately solved, and it eventually proved to be stronger than the organizational vision.

Reprinted from Joseph M. Davis, S.M., and Cyprian S. Rowe, "The Development of the National Office for Black Catholics," *U.S. Catholic Historian* 7 (1988): 269–75, with permission.

54. National Office for Black Catholics, *Black Perspectives on Evangelization of the Modern World,* 1974

The National Office for Black Catholics was established in 1970 as a bureau to work with the newly created organizations of black priests, sisters, seminarians, and laypeople as a clearinghouse and national office for planning, communication, and representation with the hierarchy, with the Holy See, and other ecclesiastical and national organizations. In 1974 under the guidance of Brother Joseph Davis, S.M., NOBC published a significant document on evangelization which antedated the apostolic exhortation Evangelii Nuntiandi *of Pope Paul VI in 1975 and the Pastoral Letter "What We Have Seen and Heard" by the black bishops of the United States in 1984.*

Introduction

As a result of growing black consciousness and the strides toward self-determination which took place in the 1960s, black people in the United States have openly and honestly assessed the implications and significance of their presence in predominantly white Christian churches, including the Roman Catholic Church. This assessment has been from a theological, philosophical, psychological and sociological perspective. The policies and practices of mainline churches, although cloaked in gospel garments, were found to be characterized by paternalism and cultural arrogance. Black people have demanded that Christian churches take new directions. This demand undoubtedly has been influenced to some extent by "secular" development, but in actuality was sparked by a sincere concern to bring about a greater consistency between the church's stated mission and its practice, particularly as it relates to a whole racial group — namely Black Americans. It is, therefore, nothing less than a call for a total revamping of the traditional notion and practice of evangelization in the black community.

Evangelization in the modern world is a topic of special importance to black Catholics in America. For us, the World Synod of Bishops presents a unique opportunity to redefine evangelization from a black perspective. We are at a point when our own thoughtful reflection on our collective experience and history in the Catholic Church must be incorporated into any contemporary blueprint for guiding Catholic ministry among black people.

For Black Catholics, considerations regarding the updating of evangelization in the black community start where revelation begins — in the culture and ethos of the people. The basis of our analysis is an awareness that **Faith** has been the sustaining force of black life in America. The traditional black church, with its emphasis on the saving presence of God throughout history, and on Christ as Liberator, has been the backbone of our constant struggle for freedom....

Definition of Evangelization

Our understanding of the mission of the People of God is derived from the Scriptures. Reading the Scriptures carefully, we find that Christ Himself frequently quoted the Old Testament as a reliable guide for discerning God's methods of instructing us.... Christ commands the apostles to evangelize the whole world, witnessing to what He has already taught, to value as He valued.... With this in mind, we are able to formulate a functional definition of evangelization.

> Evangelization is that process whereby a person is led to make a commitment to Christ, dedicate himself to a Christian mode of activity in society, and thereby become a vital member of the local church or the local community. Evangelization also involves the continuing formation of the Christian community to a conformity with Christ and the principles of the Gospel, in an attempt to bring men into a new relationship with one another through their common commitment. This community constantly extends itself, witnessing to the establishment of a new covenant — a reconstructed order, in which every man is free to live out the fullness of his God-given dignity....

The Challenge Today

It is our commitment to Christ and inner convictions about the reality of the Gospel message which produces the imperative to respond to the fact of evangelization. It demands a radical kind of commitment. On the one hand, we are encouraged by and give acknowledgement to those Blacks who, witnessing to the values of Christ, have uncompromisingly condemned the hypocrisy of the preaching the gospel through words only. Their inspiration has been the vision of a Christianity truly lived. On the other hand, we are keenly aware of the experiences of many black men and women who, acting from these same convictions, and exercising their own role in the process of evangelization, have been cautioned to prudence and patience. They have been told that in the evolution of time the Gospel will be implemented. However, the constrictions of the times in which we live tell us that "evolution — through — revolution" may be our only option.

The example of the ancient prophets, of Christ Himself, the apostles and the early fathers of the Church give us a simple lesson: false prudence and/or false patience should not be allowed to deter the total and complete witnessing of the Gospel.

We should not be comfortable in assuming that because of the centrality of the Christian faith in the past history of Black Americans the process of evangelization will be easy today. On the contrary, there are serious challenges arising from (1) the philosophical and psychological transitions which black people have undergone in recent years, as well as (2) the degrading and dehumanizing social conditions in which society continues to force us to live. The single result of both these challenges is that many black people, especially the young, question the credibility of the institution certainly, and at times Christianity itself....

The Role of the Missionary

Historically evangelization has often been used by the Church for the purpose of extending and strengthening itself as an institution. In the day-to-day practical order, the formation of the Body of Christ and the building of the Kingdom were frequently lost sight of. Because of this, missionary efforts have frequently remained static in that they have not led to the development of an indigenous local church under its own capable leadership. More often than not, missionaries became the determiners and regulators of the pace at which the local Church was permitted to evolve....

The black community of America has been interpreted ethnocentrically, as an impoverished version of the American white community. In the view of most sociologists and priests, cultural "deprivation" was thought to have induced pathogenic and dysfunctional features in the black community (cf the Moynihan Report). Ethnocentrism in the ecclesial concepts of family, love, good, strength, and values have been assumed as the yardstick for evaluating the black community. Dr. Joseph Washington has written in this framework that, "the religious expressions of the Negro have been dismissed as understandable nervous disorders," another manifestation of the pathogenic features of the community. Even the Church has laboured mistakingly [*sic*] to instill some values of "civilization" into this community.

Because of this distorted perspective, missionaries have frequently confused the proclamation of the Gospel with promulgation of their own culture. As a result, the criteria for evaluating their success or failure has too often depended on whether the people among whom they worked accepted or rejected their particular style of witness to Christ....

The National Office for Black Catholics, *Black Perspectives on Evangelization of the Modern World* (Washington, D.C.: National Office for Black Catholics, 1974), 3, 6–9, with permission.

55. Edward K. Braxton, "Toward a Black Catholic Theology," 1977

One of the foremost black Catholic theologians, Edward Braxton, now bishop of Lake Charles in Louisiana, wrote this article in 1977. In it he describes and defines the meaning of black theology in the Catholic tradition. This article is important because this was one of the first attempts to place black theology within the Catholic theological context.

There is an old saying that if you scratch the surface of one who thinks about life you will uncover a philosopher. In a similar way if you scratch the surface of one who thinks about religion you will uncover a theologian. Can it therefore be argued that if you scratch the surface of a Black Catholic who is thinking about religion in his or her context you have a Black Catholic theologian and that the product of his/her reflections constitutes a Black theology?

Theology can be defined in a host of ways. Theology may be technical philosophical reflection on the foundational questions of religion in the context of a university. By employing the methods of the academy it seeks to disclose the fundamental intelligibility of theological discourse. This may be termed foundational theology. Theology may also be technical philosophical reflection on the central themes, symbols, values of a particular church tradition in a church context. This brand of theology seeks to integrate, reinterpret and pass on the tradition that constitutes the self-concept of a religious group such as Roman Catholicism. This enterprise, sometimes apologetic in stance, may be termed systematic theology. There is yet a third possibility. Theology may be a reflection on the concrete experiential world and the wide-spread experience of oppression of various individuals and groups. In this context theology looks to the symbols of freedom and liberation that are a part of its tradition because they may provide the necessary catalysts for transforming the concrete social order. This may be called practical or pastoral theology. Very few Catholic lay persons of any hue know very much about academic or foundational theology. They simply do not have the technical skills for such an enterprise.

Most, however, do know something of practical or pastoral theology. From Sunday sermons, Catholic newspapers and periodicals they glean a conglomerate of ideas which they come to think of as "the Church view" on such issues as God, Jesus, the Church, morality, the fate of the dead, etc. Further they may be aware of the "social teachings of the Church" on war, racism, respect for life, etc., as expressed in papal encyclicals and Bishop's pastoral letters. It is no secret however that in spite of what they may be "supposed to think as Catholics" many people hold private views on almost every topic that are quite different from official teachings. Nor is this anything new. It's just being talked about more openly these days and the tensions which result from it are being exacerbated because we are in an unprecedented era of diversity and transition.

Fundamental theology has the high and distant goal of establishing a public language for discoursing about ultimate reality. Such an activity seeks to prescind from such particulars as race, sex, ethnicity, credal tradition, educational, economic and social situations. However, as you move into church or systematic theology and even more as you move into practical and pastoral theology these particulars play a very significant implicit or explicit function. Unfortunately in the Church in the past Western European, or more particularly German or Italian, theology and religious customs have been imposed on peoples of other rich heritages as if there were no room for diversity in the Catholic (i.e., open to all) Church.

Black theology is a relatively new phenomenon on the American theological scene — at least as a formal corpus. Yet its origins are as ancient as the rich religious culture of Africa and its roots are found in the pre- and post–Civil War experiences of slaves. It found beautiful expression in spirituals, sermons, blues, and stories of an oppressed people. Its contemporary spokesmen are a group of creative Protestant scholars who, as Deotis Roberts declared, "are not restrained by Catholic dogma."

While Martin Luther King, Jr., might be the admired patriarch of the present generation of Black theologians, his tempered views are not dominant in the writings of those on the scene today. In summary, they and their central themes are: a) Joseph Washington — the oppressed Blacks are God's chosen people; b) Albert Cleage — Jesus is, indeed, the Black messiah; c) J. Deotis Roberts — there is a compatibility and reconciliation with the thrust of Black liberation theology in a universal Christian vision; d) Eulalio Balthazar — White, Western theology sustains racism by supporting a color symbolism that sees white as good and black as evil; e) Major Jones — enriching Black liberation theology by constructing a Christian ethic of freedom based on agape; f) William Jones — the problem of evil framed in the compelling question, "Is God a White racist?"; g) Cecil W. Cone — an identity crisis in Black theology due to neglect of the experience of an almighty sovereign God as the point of departure for all Black theology; b) and, finally, James H. Cone, whose central theme is the joining of Black power with the biblical depiction of the God of the Exodus and the New Testament Jesus, who proclaims good news to the poor, release to captives, for the construction of a radical Black theology of liberation.

James Cone's work is probably the most systematic and he has produced the largest corpus. He insists that there are certain questions that emerge in classical Western, White theology which he considers not to be on the Black agenda. Such questions as rational arguments for the existence or non-existence of God, the christological questions of the early councils, metaphysical explanations for the problem of evil, questions about the cognitive content of biblical texts, the relationship of the assertions of religion to the advances of science — these are White questions, in Cone's view, while Black questions are those necessary for the existential survival of a people, for their liberation, their uplifting, their transformation.

I believe that this dichotomy is unfortunate. The question that must be asked is this: For which Blacks are these non-questions? Obviously those involved in the immediate struggle for survival, in past or present, are not likely to entertain metaphysical speculations. Nor are these questions for White people whose material existence is threatened. These are questions, I suggest, which in different formulations may be questions for some Black Christians, in the pews, some Black college students, some Black ministers, and some Black scholars. A key unanswered question for me is this one: What constitutes an authentic Black experience? Who constitutes the accrediting agency for genuine Blackness? Who gives the stamp of approval, if you will, to someone's postures, attitudes, points of view, as being genuinely Black?

Much as one may applaud Alex Haley's brilliant achievement in *Roots,* it remains a fact that in most cases the contemporary Black American is a peculiar hybrid of both African and European cultures. While a good case — and an urgent case — may be made that the one must be reappropriated, by what necessity do we argue that the other must be cast off, and by what process is this to be done? These and other questions must be answered if Black theology is to mature.

Such a mature enterprise might enrich the Catholic Church with a new classic. It is evident that great classics in our secular as well as our religious traditions are at once deeply personal and particular in their origins and expressions, while being at the same time public and universal in their power to transform the human spirit. Paradoxically, the profound penetration of a specific cultural, social, or religious heritage may result in an expression that is universal in its power to illuminate the human spirit. Louis Armstrong and Billie Holiday produced very particularized music forms in American jazz and blues. Yet their works are acclaimed as classics in the same manner that the symphonies of Beethoven are classics, because they have the singular capacity to touch and transform the spirit of any attentive listener.

In our culture we have a great need to experience the classic in every context, both secular and theological. Otherwise, we will have a generation of people who know nothing of Melville's *Moby Dick,* the classic story of the menacing and seductive presence of evil that can be symbolized by the sea and the sea beasts. We will have a generation that thinks Peter Benchley's

Jaws is the best sea story ever. Remarkably, and this is important, one need not have had the experience in order to be touched and transformed by the illuminating insights presented in a classic, *if* one has an attentive spirit. One need not be a member of a problem-laden Irish-American family in order to be stunned and challenged by an experience of Eugene O'Neill's *Long Day's Journey into Night*, nor need one have personal experience of the special pains and tragedies of Black urban tenement dwellers in order to participate fully in the catharsis of Lorraine Hansberry's classic play *A Raisin in the Sun*. These examples are in stark contrast to the vulgar, exploitative sensationalism found in such works as *Superfly*. Currently there is emerging a vanguard of articulate Black Catholic priests, sisters, brothers, permanent deacons, and active lay persons. Surely if these individuals begin to record their reflections on their experience of the meaning of God, Jesus, Church, worship, social responsibility and community, the whole Church would be enriched. For American Black Catholics represent a unique and often overlooked population in the Church. Because of a unique history as sons and daughters of former slaves, as converts in many cases, as pioneers on the road to full liberation in America, the reflections of Black Catholics might focus the Church anew on the meaning and purpose of religion with telling and, yes, classic urgency.

Edward K. Braxton, "Toward a Black Catholic Theology," *Freeing the Spirit* 5, no. 2, (1977): 3–6; reprinted in *Black Theology: A Documentary History, 1966–1979*, ed. Gayraud S. Wilmore and James H. Cone (Maryknoll, N.Y.: Orbis Books, 1979), 325–28, with permission.

56. The Black Catholic Theological Symposium, 1978

In October 1978, over thirty African American religious and clergy came together at the motherhouse of the Oblate Sisters of Providence to discuss the question of black theology and black Catholic theology. The participants were aware that they were embarking on a discussion that many Catholics would not understand. They were equally aware their black Protestant colleagues had contributed much to the self-understanding of American blacks at that time. Would black Catholics conclude that the Catholic tradition had no meaning for blacks? Two excerpts from the proceedings seek to articulate the meaning of the African American experience within the context of the Catholic Church.

From the Preface, by Thaddeus Posey, O.F.M. Cap.

The Black approach to theology is rooted in a positive identification and creation. It is positive because we affirm ourselves, our history and our

Father Joseph Nearon, S.S.S. (1928–84). Theologian, first director of the Institute for Black Catholic Studies at Xavier University, New Orleans. Reprinted with the permission of the Congregation of the Blessed Sacrament Archives, Cleveland.

destiny in the Faith. These are God's gifts. Until recently, the Church has not encouraged this through identification among Black Catholics. Yet the Church has always existed in, expressed herself through and identified with the cultural heritages of many nationalities, and racial groups without doing harm to her radical, God-given unity....

The question of Black Theology has for some time produced tension in the Catholic Church. This tension stems from many levels of uncertainty about both parts of the term: BLACK and THEOLOGY. Too often Black and thus black consciousness within the Church is identified with hatred, violence and separatism. Such conclusions, however, can only be reached by illogical reasoning. Theology on the other hand is too easily identified exclusively with sacred teaching (*sacra doctrina*) thereby overlooking our traditional understanding of theology as a methodical expression of the truths of divine revelation by reason, enlightened by faith. Theology is "faith seeking understanding" (*fides quaerens intellectum*). The term has for generations designated the Christian, using reason enlightened by divine faith, seeking to understand the mysteries of God revealed in his image and times past (Eph. 1–9).

Two things are required: faith and reason searching for that knowledge. This gives mankind an understanding of faith and encourages one to live faith to the fullest. God's mysteries are continually revealed to the people through Spirit (1 Cor 2:7–16). Black Theology is no more and no less than this!

Black Theology is therefore not only natural but a prerequisite to natural growth in Christ. It cannot be identified with hatred, violence and separatism. Hatred of itself places one in a negative stance before the world. Black people are not negative, our entire history of survival attests to that. Violence has never been our commitment as a people, though some segments of the community have espoused it....

Thaddeus Posey, O.F.M., Cap., Preface, *Theology: A Portrait in Black,* Proceedings of the Black Catholic Theological Symposium, Baltimore, 1978, 3, with permission.

From the Introduction, by Joseph Nearon, S.S.S.

Black Theology has a two-fold task. First, it may seek to give a black articulation of the Christian faith. Secondly, it may strive to give a Christian interpretation of the black experience. Obviously these two approaches are closely related. Yet they are not identical and the correct interpretation of any given black theologian must begin by ascertaining which of these two approaches he is taking....

The attitude of the theologian will differ because the dialectic at work in theologians of either category will differ. For both types there will be a tension between the **given** and the **criterion of interpretation**. In the first case one starts with the reality which is blackness and Christianity will be incorporated and harmonized with this reality. In the second instance one starts out with the reality which is Christian faith and strives to understand blackness in the light of this faith. The given cannot, by definition, be abandoned and this is the source of the tension. Can one be a Christian if one is black? Can one strive for black identity and black power if one is to be a faithful Christian?

I speak here of a tension, because the assumption upon which Black Theology is built is that the two poles of the tension, blackness and Christian faith, are not incompatible. Theologians who start with blackness and use it to rearticulate Christianity, emphasize that any theology which is racist, to the extent that it is racist, is in fact anti-Christian. (This is the very, very strong position of James Cone, as you well know.) Theologians who start with Christianity, seeking to find a meaning for blackness, underline that blackness is indeed meaningful, that the search for black identity is indeed legitimate precisely because of authentic Christian teaching. Both arrive at basically the same conclusion but give differing emphases and travel different paths....

...We are here because we are Black and we are here because we are Catholic theologians and we are here because we feel impelled to be close to our people and to be close to our Church.

We are here to examine our heritage in the light of our faith and to strive to articulate our faith in the light of our heritage. We do this as a contribution to our people, but we also do it as a contribution to our Church.

Joseph Nearon, S.S.S., Introduction, *Theology: A Portrait in Black,* Proceedings of the Black Catholic Theological Symposium, Baltimore, 1978, 5-6, with permission.

Part 9

THE CHURCH ADDRESSES RACISM

With the increasing momentum for a more just and humane society, the Catholic Church began to make a more forthright and direct confrontation with racial injustice both within the Church and in civil society. In the following documents the Church officially proclaimed its teaching on the essential dignity of all men and women and the basic rights due to every human being on the diocesan level, the national level, and the global level.

57. Bishop Vincent Waters Desegregates All Catholic Parishes in North Carolina, 1953

In a pastoral letter, Vincent Waters, bishop of Raleigh, North Carolina (1945–74), opened all Catholic churches to people of all races. As one of the first southern bishops to publicly desegregate his diocese, he insisted that all diocesan events be integrated. In the following pastoral letter Bishop Waters announced the end of segregation in the Church of North Carolina.

Reverend and dear Father and my dear Brethren:

The celebration of the great feast of the Sacred Heart, the Patronal Feast of our cathedral, gives me the occasion to write this to the clergy and Laity of our Diocese.

In the Diocese of Raleigh we fight only one enemy, the arch-enemy of God. No matter under what guise he may present himself or what means he might use, there is only one enemy of mankind, of the Church, and of the individual Catholic; that enemy is Satan, the arch-enemy of Christ and His Church.

The attack of the enemy is directed always against fundamentals of the Church, namely, its Unity, its Authority, its Catholicity. Men may be deceived — not a fallen angel. He knows wherein lies the strength of the Church. Whether in the entire world, in a nation, in a Diocese or in a Parish. "Divide and Conquer" has always been his plan. Divide if possible the Apostle from Christ, and from each other. Divide the faithful from the Apostles or from their priests. Divide the faithful from each other.

131

Thus divided and separated in Faith and in Communion they become an easy prey, individually or in groups, for all the other wiles of the enemy: confusion in faith and morals and eternal death is the outcome....

The enemy of God and the Church, and of mankind itself uses the "spirit of division" to break, if possible, the unity of the Mystical Body of Christ. He uses traditional hatreds of nations, of races, of classes, of minorities, of majorities, of localities, of material possessions or the need of them, to foment his divisions among men. This spirit is behind all anti-Semitism, all racial tension, all capital-labor friction, all rural-urban disputes or any other religious hatreds which have been allowed to spring up and grow in the human heart.

Opposed to all of these, and a billion times more powerful is that Love represented by the Sacred pierced Heart of Christ. It is the love for all men, who have equal opportunity to share that tremendous Love, and to return it according as they will, for it has first loved them and gone down to death for them singly and collectively.

Such a love, even more than the common hand of the Creator unites all men before God. Can men be so callous as to remember race-hatred while kneeling around the Cross of the Crucified Christ? How deceptive are the wiles of the devil. How dark are the minds of men, to his snares.

Opposed to this confusion and hatred and division, is the Church Christ founded. One Mystical Body. There can be but one, if it is Christ's as there can be but one God, and one Truth. In that one Body all the members no matter of what race, what nation, what qualities of body or of mind, or with how many or how few possessions, all are in one communion...they belong to that ONE CHURCH. Any thing to the contrary is heresy....

In North Carolina until a few years ago there were no special Catholic churches for our colored people and all Catholics worshiped God together irrespective of race. In order to give a special impetus to the missionary work among the Colored people, former bishops of Raleigh contracted with various religious communities of men and women for specialized work among these people and for the establishment of special churches and schools in some sections of the diocese for them. Did this mean that the Church was abandoning her century old teaching of "one fold and one shepherd" or that Negroes were thereby forbidden to worship in any Catholic Church in the Diocese except those for Colored? By no means. It meant that there was no division but merely that special attention was given to a few, and all Catholics still had the rights and privileges of worshiping God together, as everywhere in the Catholic Church.

To be assured that this was understood entirely by all Catholics and enforced by all Pastors, we wrote a letter clearly defining this teaching two years and a half ago on January 29, 1951. It was read in all of the churches of the Diocese and printed in the North Carolina Catholic. The same teaching has been reiterated in our letters of February 9th and May 18th of this present year.

THEREFORE, SO THAT IN THE FUTURE THERE CAN BE NO MISUNDERSTANDING ON THE PART OF ANYONE, LET ME STATE HERE AS EMPHATICALLY AS I CAN: THERE IS NO SEGREGATION OF RACES TO BE TOLERATED IN ANY CATHOLIC CHURCH IN THE DIOCESE OF RALEIGH. THE PASTORS ARE CHARGED WITH THE CARRYING OUT OF THIS TEACHING AND SHALL TOLERATE NOTHING TO THE CONTRARY. OTHERWISE, ALL SPECIAL CHURCHES FOR NEGROES SHALL BE ABOLISHED IMMEDIATELY AS LENDING WEIGHT TO THE FALSE NOTION THAT THE CATHOLIC CHURCH, THE MYSTICAL BODY OF CHRIST, IS DIVIDED. EQUAL RIGHTS ARE ACCORDED, THEREFORE, TO EVERY RACE AND EVERY NATIONALITY AS IS PROPER IN ANY CATHOLIC CHURCH. WITHIN THE CHURCH BUILDING ITSELF EVERY ONE IS GIVEN THE PRIVILEGE TO SIT OR KNEEL WHEREVER HE DESIRES AND TO APPROACH THE SACRAMENTS WITHOUT ANY REGARD TO RACE OR NATIONALITY. THIS DOCTRINE IS TO BE FULLY EXPLAINED TO EACH CONVERT WHO ENTERS THE CHURCH FROM HENCEFORTH IN THE DIOCESE OF RALEIGH....

I am not unmindful, as a Southerner, of the force of this virus of prejudice among some persons in the South, as well as in the North. I know, however, that there is a cure for this virus and that is our Faith....

The Church does not propose tolerance which is negative, but love which is positive. If Christ said love your enemies, we certainly can love our friends. These are our friends and members of our own body, the Church. It is our duty as Christians of the early days, not only to love them but to serve them. We need to help them get better educational facilities, better opportunities for culture, better living conditions, better jobs, better pay, better homes and families, better civic representation and better friendliness in the community and all of this presupposes the right to worship God freely with us in the Church everywhere....

Sincerely in the Sacred Heart of Jesus and the Immaculate Heart of Mary,

> Most Reverend Vincent S. Waters,
> Bishop of Raleigh
> Feast of the Sacred Heart of Jesus, June 12, 1953

N.B. This letter is to be read at all the Masses on Sunday, June 21st, 1953.

Reprinted from the Archives of the Diocese of Raleigh, North Carolina, with permission.

58. U.S. Bishops' Pastoral Letter on Racism, 1979

Although the question of race was one of the most bitterly fought battles in the United States during the twentieth century, the bishops of the United States were very circumspect in discussing the issues of race. In 1979, the American bishops issued a national statement that confronted racism as a moral issue that was dividing the nation and destroying the well-being of the country.

Racism is a sin: a sin that divides the human family, blots out the image of God among specific members of that family, and violates the fundamental human dignity of those called to be children of the same Father. Racism is the sin that says some human beings are inherently superior and others essentially inferior because of race. It is the sin that makes racial characteristics the determining factor for the exercise of human rights. It mocks the words of Jesus: "Treat others the way you would have them treat you" (Matthew 7:12). Indeed, racism is more than a disregard for the words of Jesus; it is a denial of the truth of the dignity of each human being revealed by the mystery of the Incarnation....

When we give in to our fears of the other because he or she is of a race different from ourselves, when we prejudge the motives of others precisely because they are of a different color, when we stereotype or ridicule the other because of racial characteristics and heritage, we fail to heed the command of the Prophet Amos: "Seek good and not evil, that you may live; then truly will the Lord...be with you as you claim!...Then let justice surge like water, and goodness like an unfailing stream" (Amos 5:14, 24).

Today in our country men, women, and children are being denied opportunities for full participation and advancement in our society because of their race. The educational, legal, and financial systems, along with other structures and sectors of our society, impede people's progress and narrow their access because they are black, Hispanic, Native American or Asian.

The structures of our society are subtly racist, for these structures reflect the values which society upholds. They are geared to the success of the majority and the failure of the minority. Members of both groups give unwitting approval by accepting things as they are. Perhaps no single individual is to blame. The sinfulness is often anonymous but nonetheless real. The sin is social in nature in that each of us, in varying degrees, is responsible. All of us in some measure are accomplices.... "The absence of personal fault for an evil does not absolve one of all responsibility. We must seek to resist and undo injustices we have not caused, lest we become bystanders who tacitly endorse evil and so share in guilt for it" [quoting from *To Live in Christ Jesus* (Washington, D.C.: NCCB, 1976), 25].

How great, therefore, is that sin of racism which weakens the Church's witness as the universal sign of unity among all peoples! How great the scandal given by racist Catholics who would make the Body of Christ, the Church, a sign of racial oppression! Yet all too often the Church in our country has been for many a "white Church," a racist institution.

Each of us as Catholics must acknowledge a share in the mistakes and sins of the past. Many of us have been prisoners of fear and prejudice. We have preached the Gospel while closing our eyes to the racism it condemns. We have allowed conformity to social pressures to replace compliance with social justice....

Therefore, let the Church proclaim to all that the sin of racism defiles the image of God and degrades the sacred dignity of humankind which has been revealed by the mystery of the Incarnation. Let all know that it is a terrible sin that mocks the cross of Christ and ridicules the Incarnation. For the brother and sister of our Brother Jesus Christ are brother and sister to us....

> "Brothers and Sisters to Us," United States Catholic Bishops' Pastoral Letter on Racism in Our Day (Washington, D.C.: United States Catholic Conference, 1979), with permission.

59. Black Bishops of the United States, Pastoral Letter on Evangelization, 1984

Their pastoral letter What We Have Seen and Heard *was the first written by the black bishops of the United States to black Catholics in the United States. The ten active black bishops in the United States sought to remind the black Catholic community that black Catholics were no longer dependents but adults, responsible for the evangelization of fellow blacks and contributors to the Catholic Church in the United States.*

Within the history of every Christian community there comes the time when it reaches adulthood. This maturity brings with it the duty, the privilege and the joy to share with others the rich experience of the "Word of Life...."

We, the ten Black bishops of the United States, chosen from among you to serve the People of God, are a significant sign among many other signs that the Black Catholic community in the American Church has now come of age. We write to you as brothers that "you may share life with us." We write also to all those who by their faith make up the People of God in the United States that "our joy may be complete...."

Evangelization is both a call and a response. It is the call of Jesus reverberating down the centuries: "Go into the whole world and proclaim the good news to all creation" (Mark 16:15). The response is "Conduct your-selves, then, in a way worthy of the gospel of Christ" (Philippians 1:27). Evangelization means not only preaching but witnessing; not only conversion but renewal; not only entry into the community but the building up of the community; not only hearing the Word but sharing it....

Pope Paul VI issued that call to the peoples of Africa when he said to them at Kampala in Uganda, "You are now missionaries to yourselves...." And Pope Paul also laid out for all sons and daughters of Africa the nature of the response: "You must now give your gifts of Blackness to the whole Church."

We believe that these solemn words of our Holy Father Paul VI were addressed not only to Africans today but also to us, the children of the Africans of yesterday. We believe that the Holy Father has laid a challenge before us to share the gift of our Blackness with the Church in the United States. This is a challenge to be evangelizers, and so we want to write about this gift which is also a challenge....

Black Americans are a people rich with spiritual gifts....Black Spirituality has four major characteristics. It is contemplative. It is holistic. It is joyful. It is communitarian....

Black Spirituality is contemplative. By this we mean that prayer is spontaneous and pervasive in the Black tradition. Every place is a place for prayer because God's presence is heard and felt in every place. Black Spirituality senses the awe of God's transcendence and the vital intimacy of his closeness. God's power breaks into the "sin-sick world" of everyday. The sense of God's presence and power taught our ancestors that no one can run from him and no one need hide from him....

Black Spirituality, in contrast with much of Western tradition, is holistic. Like the biblical tradition, there is no dualism. Divisions between intellect and emotion, spirit and body, action and contemplation, individual and community, sacred and secular are foreign to us. In keeping with our African heritage, we are not ashamed of our emotions. For us, the religious experience is an experience of the whole human being — both the feelings and the intellect, the heart as well as the head. Moreover, we find foreign any notion that the body is evil. We find our own holistic spiritual approach to be in accord with the Scriptures and the logic of the Incarnation....

Joy is a hallmark of Black Spirituality. Joy is first of all celebration. Celebration is movement and song, rhythm and feeling, color and sensation, exultation and thanksgiving. We celebrate the presence and the proclamation of the Word.

This joy is a sign of our faith and especially our hope. It is never an escape from reality, however harsh it may be. Indeed this joy is often present even in the midst of deep anguish and bitter tears....

One who is joyful is impelled to love and cannot hate. A joyful person seeks to reconcile and will not cause division. A joyful person is troubled by the sign of another's sadness. A joyful person seeks to console, strives to encourage and brings to all true peace.

Such is the gift so clearly needed in our time. Such is the gift that Jesus passed on to us on the evening he died....

In African culture the "I" takes its meaning in the "we." In other words, individual identity is to be found within the context of the community. Even today, Black Christianity is eminently a social reality. The sense of community is a major component of Black Spirituality....

The communal dimension of Black Spirituality permeates our experience of liturgy and worship. Worship must be shared. Worship is always a celebration of community. No one stands in prayer alone. One prays and acts within and for the community. Each one supports, encourages and enriches the other and is in turn enriched, encouraged and supported....

Through the liturgy, Black people will come to realize that the Catholic Church is a homeland for Black believers just as she is for people of other cultural and ethnic traditions. In recent years, remarkable progress has been made in our country by many talented Black experts to adapt the liturgy to the needs and the genius of the African-American community. In order that this work can be carried on more fully within the Catholic tradition and at the same time be enriched by our own cultural heritage, we wish to recall the essential qualities that should be found in a liturgical celebration within the Black Catholic community. It should be authentically Black. It should be truly Catholic. And it should be well prepared and well executed.

"What We Have Seen and Heard," A Pastoral Letter on Evangelization from the Black Bishops of the United States (Cincinnati: St. Anthony Messenger Press, 1984), with permission.

60. Pontifical Commission for Justice and Peace, Statement on Racism, 1988

This document is the first document from the Holy See specifically addressing racism. It was issued by the Pontifical Commission for Justice and Peace, which was created in 1976 by Pope Paul VI. The document was issued to state the Church's view on racial strife and division worldwide.

Introduction

Racial prejudice or racist behavior continues to trouble relations between persons, human groups and nations. Public opinion is increasingly incensed by it. Moral conscience can by no means accept it. The Church is especially sensitive to this discriminatory attitude. The message which she has drawn from biblical Revelation strongly affirms the dignity of every person created in God's image, the unity of humankind in the Creator's plan, and the dynamics of the reconciliation worked by Christ the Redeemer who has broken down the dividing wall which kept opposing worlds apart in order to recapitulate all persons in him.

For this reason, the Holy Father asked the Pontifical Commission "Iustitia et Pax" to help enlighten and awaken consciences about this major concern: namely, the reciprocal respect between ethnic and racial groups as well as their fraternal coexistence. Such a task presupposes a lucid analysis of complex situations of both past and present, as well as an unbiased judgment about moral shortcomings and positive initiatives, in the light of fundamental ethical principles and the Christian message. Christ denounced evil, even at the risk of his life. He did this not to condemn but to save. Likewise, the Holy See feels that it has the duty to denounce deplorable situations prophetically. In so doing, it is careful, however, not to condemn or exclude persons. It wants, rather, to help them find a way out of such situations through concrete and progressive efforts. It wishes, with all due realism, to reinforce the hope of renewal, which is always possible, and to propose suitable pastoral guidelines for Christians and all people of good will who seek the same objectives....

Racist Behavior throughout History

Historically, racial prejudice, in the strict sense of the word, that is, awareness of the biologically determined superiority of one's own race or ethnic group with respect to others, developed above all from the practice of colonization and slavery at the dawn of the modern era....

With the *discovery of the New World, attitudes changed.* The first great wave of European colonization was, in fact, accompanied by a massive destruction of pre-Columbian civilizations and a brutal enslavement of their peoples. If the great navigators of the fifteenth and sixteenth centuries were free from racial prejudices, the soldiers and traders did not have the same respect for others: they killed in order to take possession of the land, reduced first the "Indians" and then the blacks to slavery in order to exploit their work.

At the same time, they began to develop a racist theory in order to justify their actions....

In the context of racial contempt — although the motive was primarily to obtain cheap labor — mention must be made of the *slave trade* of blacks from Africa, bought by the hundreds of thousands and brought to the Americas. Their capture and traveling conditions were such that many died, even before their departure or their arrival in the New World. There they were destined to the most menial tasks, to all intents and purposes as slaves. This trade began in 1562 and the slavery that resulted was to last nearly three centuries. Here once again, the Popes and theologians, at the same time as numerous humanists, rose up against this practice. Leo XIII vigorously denounced it in his Encyclical *In plurimis* of 5 May 1888, in which he congratulated Brazil for having abolished slavery. The publication of this present document coincides with the *centenary of that memorable Charter.* John Paul II, in his speech to African intellectuals in Yaoundé (13 August 1985), did not hesitate to deplore the fact that persons belonging to Christian nations had contributed to the black slave trade....

In the eighteenth century, a veritable *racist theology*, opposed to the teaching of the Church, was forged. It stood in contrast, moreover, with the commitment of some humanist philosophers who promoted the dignity and freedom of the black slaves, at that time the object of a shameless and wide-spread trade. This racist ideology believed it could find the justification for its prejudices in *science*. Apart from the difference in physical characteristics and skin color, it sought to deduce an essential difference, of a hereditary biological nature, in order to affirm that the subjugated peoples belonged to intrinsically inferior "races" with regard to their mental, moral or social qualities. It was at the end of the eighteenth century that the word "race" was used for the first time to classify human beings biologically. In the following century, we can even find an interpretation of the history of civilizations in biological terms, as a contest between strong races and weak ones, with the latter being genetically inferior to the former. The decadence of the major civilizations was explained by their "degeneration" — i.e., the mixing of races which weakened the purity of blood.

Forms of Racism Today

Today racism has not disappeared. There are even troubling new manifestations of it here and there in various forms, be they spontaneous, officially tolerated or institutionalized. In fact, if cases of segregation based on racial theories are the exception in today's world, the same cannot be said about phenomena of exclusion or aggressivity. The victims are certain groups of persons whose physical appearance or ethnic, cultural or religious characteristics are different from those of the dominant group, and are interpreted by the latter as being signs of an innate and definitive inferiority, thereby justifying all discriminatory practices in their regard. If, in fact, race defines a human group in terms of immutable and hereditary physical traits, racist prejudice, which dictates racist behavior, can be applied by extension, with equally negative effects, to all persons whose ethnic origin, language, religion or customs make them appear different....

Contribution of Christians, in Union with Others, to Promoting Fraternity and Solidarity amongst Races

Racial prejudice, which denies the equal dignity of the members of the human family and blasphemes the Creator, can only be eradicated by going to its roots, where it is formed: *in the human heart.* It is from the heart that just or unjust behavior is born, according to whether persons are open to God's will — in the natural order and in the Living Word — or whether they close themselves up in those egoisms dictated by fear or the instinct of domination. It is the way we look at others that must be purified. Harboring racist thoughts and entertaining racist attitudes is a sin against the specific message of Christ for whom one's "neighbor" is not only a person from my tribe, my milieu, my religion or my nation: it is every person that I meet along the way....

> Pontifical Commission Iustitia et Pax, *The Church and Racism: Towards a More Fraternal Society* (Vatican City, 1988; Washington, D.C.: Office of Publishing and Promotion Services, United States Catholic Conference, 1988), with permission.

61. Statement on the Tenth Anniversary of the Black Bishops' Letter on Racism, 1989

To observe the tenth anniversary of the publication of Brothers and Sisters to Us: U.S. Bishops' Pastoral Letter on Racism in Our Day, *the Bishops' Committee on Black Catholics published a statement on the presence of racism in the United States in 1989.*

Today, both individual and corporate institutional racism is on the rise in our country. We experience and hear about blatant forms of racism on the campuses of our colleges and universities — Catholic colleges are not exempt. In our cities, in government agencies, in the political arena, in corporate board rooms and, in some instances, in our church-related high schools and elementary schools, the ugly head of racism surfaces. During the past eight years, ground has been lost and hard-won civil rights have suffered greatly due to a lack of legislative support. False and misleading information about affirmative action initiatives and practices was fed to the public, with our apology. Housing developers and real estate agencies, along with many municipalities, adopted exclusionary policies and practices, even in defiance of state and federal regulations. It has been discovered that some of the most active Ku Klux Klan members are Catholics. Neo-Nazis, young and old, enjoy a resurgence that is hard to understand....

The reality of racism in 1989 vis à vis theological considerations on the subject forcefully challenges our consciousness. In spite of all that has been said and written about racism in the last twenty years, very little — if anything at all — has been done in Catholic education; such as it was yesterday, it is today....

This Special Message is not meant to repeat what *Brothers and Sisters to Us* has said, nor what the pontifical document paints in much broader strokes. The purpose is to share in some small way, our hopes, disappointments, joys, and pain — perhaps, too, in a larger way our faith. We do have faith in good people everywhere in this country who would care, if only they knew. If only they would become conscious of the devastation, the tragedies, and the alienation, especially in the Church, that racism has caused and is causing. Good people would react positively if they realized, too, that *freedom for the victims of racism is a right-to-life issue*. We believe that good women and men would come together and profess, if only to themselves, their racism — conscious or otherwise.

Bishops' Committee on Black Catholics/National Conference of Catholic Bishops, *For the Love of One Another: A Special Message on the Occasion of the Tenth Anniversary of "Brothers and Sisters to Us"* (Washington, D.C.: United States Catholic Conference, 1989), 40–42, with permission.

.

Part 10

THE WITNESS OF
AFRICAN AMERICAN CATHOLICS:
CHALLENGE AND HOPE

African American Catholics have given a witness to the American community as a whole and to the white Catholic community in particular. This witness is one of undying faith over four centuries. In many other ways African American Catholics have had a major influence on the spiritual and liturgical life of the Catholic community.

62. Clarence Rivers, "The Gift of Music," 2001

African Americans have given to the Catholic Church distinctive art forms in their music and in the vibrant style of liturgical celebration that was brought from Africa and reborn in the world of the African Diaspora. One of those who had an enormous impact on post–Vatican II music was Clarence Rivers, a black priest of the archdiocese of Cincinnati. In 1964, his song "God Is Love" took the African idiom and made it everybody's song. In the following document, Father Rivers recounts his development as a liturgist and a musician.

As a newly ordained minister (1956) and associate pastor to Msgr. Clement J. Busemeyer at St. Joseph's Parish in the West End of Cincinnati, I expected this exteriorly gruff, Teutonic pastor to be unconcerned about the *quality* of worship; his masses took from twenty to thirty minutes.... However, he was very much concerned that worship was not reaching and touching the people in the pews. One day he said to me, "People are coming to church only because they're afraid of *catching hell*, if they don't." He then pointedly asked, "Can you do something about this?" His clumsy question is much more vivid in memory than my crazy response, which, I believe, was an unequivocal, though naïve, "Yes, I think I can! I can do something about THIS...."

Fr. Busemeyer had also indicated that he saw a place for Black music in the Catholic Church. He lamented the fact that the archbishop had not allowed a concert of Negro music at the (not yet restored) cathedral. My own interpretation of this was that there should be a place for all Black religious culture in worship. Around the same time Fr. Boniface Luykx, a Belgian Norbertine monk, on his way going to or coming from his annual courses in liturgy taught at Notre Dame, began to stop off in Cincinnati. On one occasion he challenged Giles Harry Pater, a very dear friend of mine, and me to start composing music for the liturgy out of our own backgrounds. There was nothing wrong with challenging Harry; he was a trained, educated musician. But there was a danger in challenging me: I did not know enough to know that I could not compose. Or closer to the truth, I really believed that musical compositions, especially with words, must be as natural as speaking a language even before becoming literate in that language. So I accepted the challenge....

One Sunday afternoon I was returning from Virginia Beach where I had delivered a speech on race relations. I was not yet used to flying, and, I must say, Piedmont Airlines' little prop jet did not inspire confidence. We were flying over the Appalachian mountains during a thunderstorm. I took out my (before-its-time) English language breviary and started to read the Sunday Office. I was struck with the words of St. John: "God is love; and he who abides in love abides in God; and God in him." I started applying a melody and a musical rhythm to the piece, mostly in my head, and possibly humming very softly to myself and occasionally scrawling lines and dots as pegs to my memory. I repeated the melody incessantly in my head...almost unconsciously, a change in American church music had begun....

Had I not been in Washington I would never have come into contact with the official and unofficial leadership of the Liturgical Conference, nor would I have been privileged to sit on its board. I might never have been invited to share my "new" music with the American Church at the meeting of the Liturgical Conference in St. Louis at Kiel Auditorium in August of 1964. The Conference convened some twenty thousand strong for the first Mass in English.

As I remember it, I was only on the program to lead one communion hymn. The song was "God Is Love" (the very first I ever composed). The music so energized the crowd, however, that I was called back, again and again, to share more of the music with the assembly. And lucky us, the Purcell High School Mafia...was there to sell thousands of our album, *An American Mass Program*.... At the conference in St. Louis I was made into an instant celebrity. All I did was smile and shake hands and try to answer all sorts of questions that I was ill equipped to handle. I retreated to my hotel room at night, unable to remove the frozen smile from my face and relax my aching right hand....

Clarence-Rufus J. Rivers, "Freeing the Spirit: Very Personal Reflections on One Man's Search for the Spirit in Worship," *U.S. Catholic Historian* 19 (2001): 97–99, 107–8, with permission.

63. Bryan Massingale, "The African American Experience and United States Roman Catholic Ethics," 1997

Among the black Catholic theologians who have begun to look at theological questions from a non-European and non-American perspective is Father Bryan Massingale, professor at St. Francis Seminary in Milwaukee, Wisconsin. In his critique of current issues discussed by Catholic ethicists, Massingale shows that American Catholic ethicists have practically ignored all questions regarding racism or the morality of racial segregation and practices. Father Massingale takes this occasion to look at Catholic social ethics from the perspective of an African American theologian.

A review of the "Notes" [on moral theology in the journal *Theological Studies*] from 1970 [onwards]...reveals virtually no mention of — and certainly no sustained attention to — the reality of racism or race relations. One searches...in vain for in-depth reflection on events such as the Black Power Movement, the open housing marches, the debates over affirmative action, or the racial conflagrations of 1965, 1967, and 1968. Thus the Civil Rights Movement, the catalyst for some of the most epochal social changes in U.S. history, passed unnoticed by American Catholic moralists who were consumed by other matters — specifically, the controversies surrounding the morality of artificial contraception....

I cannot help but notice that in Catholic moral discourse, blacks are treated as the *objects* of white study, analysis, and charity — and rarely seen as *subjects* capable of independent action or creative initiative which can shape white response. To put it another way, there is no acknowledgment of black *agency*; black people are usually acted upon, seldom the actors, in Catholic moral discourse. Such a view cannot but render Catholic ethical reflection in matters of race inadequate and impoverished, if not absolutely erroneous....

It would be an injustice to ignore the exceptions which exist in this pattern of omission, silence, neglect, and indifference to racial concerns in the U.S. Catholic moral academy. One cannot overlook the efforts of John LaFarge, Joseph Leonard, and Daniel Maguire. Nor should one fail to mention the 1979 pastoral letter of the U.S. Bishops on racism, *Brothers and Sisters to Us*. Yet such works are truly the "exceptions which prove the rule." Thus, the conclusion is obvious and inescapable: the moral aspects of race relations have not been, and still are not, a major concern or significant interest of American Catholic ethicists. Documentable history does not support any other judgment. Indeed, to state that racial justice is of peripheral interest to the moral academy may well be an overstatement. Hence, the task or goal of establishing a dialogue between the African

American experience and U.S. Catholic moral theology has to surmount a major difficulty: the lack of a dialogue partner...indeed, the absence of any significant evidence of interest on the part of American Catholic ethicists in what is arguably the most persistent and insidious human rights issue in America....

A final feature of African American religious ethics to be considered is that it is an ethic of hope. Hope is an essential requirement for an oppressed people yearning and striving for justice. Thus black religious ethics must be guided by a vision capable of inspiring and instilling that hope which can motivate and sustain a people in the face of the difficult, persistent, often elusive and perhaps permanent quest for freedom, justice, and equality — for full recognition as human beings.

African American ethicists usually articulate this hope in biblical images and metaphors....

[James Cone] proposes that the image of "Pentecost" can serve as a vehicle for conveying a vision of hope capable of guiding and sustaining reflection and action toward the goal of a racially just and inclusive society. In the Pentecost narrative, all the peoples of the earth heard the Good News preached in their own tongues. Viewed from this perspective, "Pentecost" becomes a metaphor for cultural pluralism and diversity, the divine grounding for the acceptance of religious basis for moving toward a pluralistic solution to the question of racial justice, a solution which envisions full participation and inclusion combined with a respect for cultural identity. Thus "Pentecost" can serve as a biblical image of hope, sustaining ethical reflection and action which both critiques the present and strives to create a new social order: a society governed by the canons of neither "integration," nor "assimilation," nor "separation," but rather those of "transformation," the affirmation of difference, and the embrace of plural models of what is accepted as "American" — or indeed "human."

Bryan Massingale, "The African American Experience and U.S. Roman Catholic Ethics: 'Strangers and Aliens No Longer?' in *Black and Catholic: The Challenge and Gift of Black Folk*, ed. Jamie T. Phelps (Milwaukee: Marquette University Press, 1997), 82, 84, 86, 92–93, with permission.

64. M. Shawn Copeland, "Catholic Theology: African American Context," 1998

Black Catholic theologians have emerged into the new millennium as serious scholars in the world of Catholic learning. Black Catholic theologians, like Hispanic, African, and Asian theologians, have begun to demonstrate how the Catholic tradition embraces all peoples and cultures. Doctor

Shawn Copeland of Boston University and the Institute of Black Catholic Studies at Xavier University in New Orleans has used the methodological approach of Bernard Lonergan to lay the basis of a Catholic theology in an African American context.

Reflection on method in emerging black Catholic theology provokes several questions. On the one hand, one of the most blatant misunderstandings about Catholic theology is that it merely repeats what the magisterium dictates; on the other hand, one of the most blatant misunderstandings about black theology is that it is turned-in on itself and displays little concern for objective criteria. How is an authentic black Catholic theology to discredit such disinformation? How is an authentic black theology to respond to the demanding set of traditions related to the magisterium or teaching authority of the Roman Catholic Church? By whose or what authority does the black Catholic theologian speak? If black theologies insist on the authoritative character of the black experience, how are we to understand authority? How are we to understand "black experience"? To whom or to what is the black Catholic theologian accountable? For whom and for what is she or he responsible?

These questions, although difficult, are not necessarily antagonistic. Rather, they form a crucial aspect of the *locus theologicus* of black Catholic theology. Indeed, our cultural, existential, and ecclesial situation as African American Catholic theologians is compound-complex. That situation obliges us to contest the imputation of the patently false dichotomy between black and Catholic. It requires us to excavate, critique, and reconstruct our African-derived religious, cultural, and aesthetic wisdom, traditions, and practices. At the same time, because our formal theological preparation constitutes both spiritual and discursive formation, we black Catholic theologians engage and are engaged by a liturgical, spiritual, and intellectual tradition nearly two thousand years old. Further, because our situatedness in the Americas is the result of brutal betrayal and calloused enslavement, we black Catholic theologians and scholars are challenged to critically appropriate the religions, cultures, and histories that shape our distinctive heritage.

This triangulation — religio-cultural Africanisms, Catholic faith, American history — demands that our communal and individual intellectual praxis transcend and transform boundaries imputed to us. It further discloses the importance and power of identity and identity formation. Thus, a determinative aspect of the *locus theologicus,* or the place from which we do black Catholic theology, is our despised black identity....

Self-definition is, above all, a human task and obligation. To name ourselves, our history, culture, intellectual and social movements, and Catholic religious praxis "black" is an act of self-determination, defiance, and courage. When we do this, we acknowledge and embrace an identity that has been shaped under duress, anxiety, and rejection in society and in our church. When we call ourselves and our enterprise "black Catholic," we are not repudiating the universal nature and mission of our church; rather, we are giving a name to our particularity, to our gift and presence within it. In conformity with our baptismal vocation, we are naming ourselves *as* church — not something to which we belong, but who *we are*....

Our struggle "to be church," not merely "to belong," has placed us black Catholics and black Catholic theology on the horns of a dilemma. On the one hand, the moral integrity of black Catholicism and the theology that would mediate it requires an unequivocal rejection of segregation in any form. As members of the Body of Christ, we too desire to live as Jesus lived, to put our communal and personal, cultural and social decisions at the service of the coming Reign of God. On the other hand, pastoral neglect and disregard by white clergy and hierarchy have forced black Catholics to seek out separate sites for the development of our own spiritual life. Must we, as full baptized members of the church, as members of the Body of Christ, relinquish our desire and attempt to live a life worthy of our Christian calling? This struggle to be church, to be authentically black and truly Catholic, is most poignant, for our tendencies toward authentic integration, inclusion, and participation historically have proved dangerous for black Catholic initiatives. The thwarted work of the black Catholic congresses of the nineteenth century, the collapse of the Federated Colored Catholics in the early twentieth century, the demise of Catholic schools in so many cities, along with the mergers and closures of so many parishes that nurtured black Catholics challenge our current Black Catholic Congress movement to reflect more deeply on our situation. In this endeavor the work of black Catholic theologians and scholars will be crucial....

M. Shawn Copeland, "Method in Emerging Black Catholic Theology," in *Taking Down Our Harps: Black Catholics in the United States*, ed. Diana L. Hayes and Cyprian Davis (Maryknoll, N.Y.: Orbis Books, 1988), 120–22, 134–35, with permission.

65. Thea Bowman, "Voice of the People, Voice of an Age," 1985

Teacher, gospel singer, evangelist, prophet, Sister Thea Bowman, F.S.P.A., addressed the issue of racial prejudice and injustice with charismatic presence bolstered by rare talents in song, sermon, and story. She sought to help African American Catholics discover their Catholic roots and their black

roots at a time when black Americans were learning about the disintegra-
tion of the African American family. Sister Thea reaches into the black family
tradition of the South to celebrate and challenge black families today.

Introduction

This book is by Black people from Black families for Black people from Black families.

It assumes that the Black family is alive and well. It assumes further that we as a people need to find ways old and new to walk and talk together; to bond more surely; to extend family more widely and effectively, so that no one is fatherless, motherless, sisterless, or brotherless; so that no one lacks the life sustaining human support of family.

Sister Thea Bowman, F.S.P.A. (1937–90). Teacher, evangelist, diocesan consultant for intercultural affairs in Jackson, Mississippi. Reprinted with permission of the Archives of the Franciscan Sisters of Perpetual Adoration, La Crosse, Wisconsin

It attempts to help us maintain and strengthen Black rootedness, Black traditions and rituals whereby faith and values are transmitted and celebrated in family, in extended family, in intimate person-to-person exchange — mother to son, grandchild to grandpa, play brother to younger sister, friend to friend, member to member, and family to family. And whereby faith and values are transmitted and celebrated in casual conversation, in reminiscence and testimony, in song and dance, and in ritual and story.

It encourages Black families to think and talk about ourselves; our faith; our lived experience of family, Blackness, and Catholicism. It encourages us to think and talk about our dreams, goals, and aspirations; our concrete plans for being family and community, and for sharing our gift of Blackness with the Church....

Too often, white people come to us with the answers to our problems. They don't bother to try to find out who we are, how we think, and what we're about. Too often, people who come to help do not realize that Black family is alive and well and that even when broken, even when hurting, it fosters deep faith and forges strong bonds....

The Challenges

                stress
            loneliness frustration worry
          anxiety obsession oppression
        repression depression bills inflation
            insecurity poverty unemployment underemployment
      layoffs rip-offs last-hired first fired
                    injustice unequal opportunity
  systematic exclusion from full participation in political,
        social, educational, economic, and
                    religious organizations and institutions
          inadequate education inadequate housing
        homelessness inadequate health care
      inadequate sanitation inadequate nutrition
        retardation senility starvation aggression
      violence crime murder rape robbery incest conflict
  economic conflict religious conflict family conflict
            crime black-on-black crime jail
        imprisonment police brutality violence
      family violence child abuse wife abuse husband abuse
            teen-age pregnancies unwanted pregnancies

abortion frustration alcohol abuse drug abuse
chemical dependency illness accident hypochondria
dependency agency dependency delinquency
street gangs rumbles wars drop-outs cop-outs run-aways
hustlers dealers pimping prostitution
separation death suicide mobility upward mobility
materialism consumerism elitism classism racism sexism
manipulation exploitation anxiety loneliness
stress

Thea Bowman, ed., *Families, Black and Catholic, Catholic and Black: Readings, Resources, and Family Activities* (Washington, D.C.: United States Catholic Conference, 1985), 11, 32, with permission.

66. Diana L. Hayes, Voice of Womanists, 1998

Diana L. Hayes, theologian, attorney, writer, and professor at Georgetown University, has helped to define the theological voice of black women and to differentiate it from that of white women. Here Hayes presents us with Mary, the Mother of God, as "Woman who was poor" and also black.

As active participants in the ongoing dialogue among Black theologians, male and female, Protestant and Catholic, and having experienced for ourselves the tri- and even quadra-dimensional situation of being Black, Catholic, female, and poor, we are privileged, so to speak, to serve as a nexus for an emerging Black Catholic womanist theology. It is here that womanist theology and Black theology converge in the voices of women who have been oppressed because of their race, their gender, their class, and their faith....

It is, perhaps, in their reinterpretation of the role and presence of Mary, the mother of God, that Black Catholic women can make the most significant contribution. Too often seen as a docile, submissive woman, Black Catholic womanists, instead, see a young woman sure of her God and of her role in God's salvific plan. She is a woman who, in her song (Luke 46:1–55), proclaims her allegiance with God and with her brothers and sisters with whom she lived, as a Jew under Roman oppression, a poor and marginalized existence similar to the existence of Blacks in the church for so long. They relate to her by sharing in her experiences as women who are also oppressed but who continue to bear the burden of faith and to pass on their faith to generations to come. At a time when women were supposed to be silent and invisible, when women were considered of little importance, Mary accepted a singular call from God to stand out as "blessed among all women." As a

young, pregnant, unwed woman who had many difficult questions to answer within her community, she still had the courage to say a powerful and
prophetic "yes" to God that shattered all of time. She is a role model, not for
passivity, but for strong, righteous, "womanish" women who spend their
lives giving birth to the future. As Black Catholic women, we challenge our
church to recognize the legitimacy of our presence within it and our calling
as baptized in Christ to serve the church as the people of God....

Diana L. Hayes, "And When We Speak: To Be Black, Catholic, and Womanist," in
Taking Down Our Harps: Black Catholics in the United States, ed. Diana L. Hayes
and Cyprian Davis (Maryknoll, N.Y.: Orbis Books, 1998), 113–14; originally in
Diana L. Hayes, *And Still We Rise: An Introduction to Black Liberation Theology*
(Mahwah, N.J.: Paulist Press, 1996), with permission.

INDEX

education (*continued*)
  Black Catholic Congresses on, 81, 82
  contrast of Protestant and Catholic
    work on blacks', 91–92
  founding of an order of black sisters in
    Georgia and, 94–95
  Slattery on the, of priests, 67–70
Elder, Archbishop William Henry,
  32–35, 78
England, Bishop John, 28–30, 35
Epiphany College, 67, 69
ethics, 145–46
ethnocentrism, 123
evangelization, 121–23, 135–37

families, black, 149–51
Faustina, Gilbert, 97–98
Federated Colored Catholics, 90, 92
foundational/fundamental theology,
  124, 125
Franciscan Handmaids of Mary, 94–96
fraternal organizations, 96–97
freed slaves, 3–5, 11–12
Friendship House, 108
fugitive slaves, 11

Gaudin, Juliette, 51, 52
Gotti, Cardinal Girolamo Maria, 87
Gregory XVI, Pope, 35, 37, 38–40
Grey, Sister Martin de Porres, 118
Gunn, Right Reverend John E., 99

Harlem Renaissance, the, 103, 107
Hayes, Diana L., 151–52
Healy, Alexander Sherwood, 58, 59
Healy, Bishop James Augustine, 58,
  59–60
Healy, Patrick Francis, S.J., 58
*The History of the Black Catholics in the
  United States* (Davis), xiii
Hughes, Archbishop John J., 30

In Supremo Apostolatus Fastigio, 38–40

Janser, Peter, 98–101
Jesuits, 88
John II (king of Aragon), 3
Jones, Major, 125

Jones, William, 125
Josephites. *See* Society of St. Joseph of
  the Sacred Heart
Joubert de la Muraille, Jacques, 47

King, Martin Luther, Jr., 111, 125
Knights of Peter Claver, 96–98

Ladies of Peter Claver, 96
LaFarge, John, 91, 145
laity, the, 79–83, 90–94, 96–97
Lambert, Rollins, 119
Lange, Elizabeth, 18, 18n.4, 47
Lavigerie, Cardinal, 78, 79
Leonard, Joseph, 145
Leo XII, Pope, 21
liberation theology. *See* black theology
Lissner, Ignatius, 94–96
liturgy, 143–44
Louis XIV (king of France), 7
Louisiana, 6–12
Lucas, Lawrence, 116–17

Maguire, Daniel, 145
Malcolm X, 116–17
Markoe, William, 91
marriage, 9–10, 20–22
Marshall, Thurgood, 111
Martin, Bishop Auguste, 35–36
Mary (mother of Jesus), 151–52
Massingale, Bryan, 145–46
McKay, Claude, 103–7, 108
militant protest, 112
Mill Hill Fathers, 64, 67
mixed marriage, 9
moral theology, 145
mulattos, 13
music, liturgical, 143–44
mutual benevolent societies, 22–24

National Black Catholic Clergy Caucus,
  111–14, 116, 118–23
National Black Sisters' Conference,
  114–16, 118, 120
National Conference of Catholic
  Bishops, 120
nationalism, black, 118